THE OAKWOOD LIBRARY OF RAILWAY HISTORY   OL165

The Mansfield Railway

*Serving 'Old King Coal',
'Fast Fish'
and
holidays at the seaside*

*by
Robert Western*

THE OAKWOOD PRESS

© Oakwood Press & Robert Western 2019

Published by Oakwood Press, an imprint of Stenlake Publishing Ltd, in 2019, reprinted with minor corrections in 2022

British Library Cataloguing in Publication Data
A Record for this book is available from the British Library
ISBN 978 0 85361 603 0

Printed by Blissetts, Unit E1-E8 Shield Drive, West Cross Industrial Park, Brentford, TW8 9EX

All rights reserved. No part of this book may be reproduced or transmitted in any form or by any means, electronic or mechanical, including photocopying, recording or by any information storage and retrieval system, without permission from the Publisher in writing.

By the same author

The Ingleton Branch, Oakwood Press, 1990 (Revised Edition, 2018)
   (First published as *The Lowgill Branch,* Oakwood, 1971)
The Eden Valley Railway, Oakwood Press, 1997 (Revised Edition, 2014)
The Cockermouth Keswick and Penrith Railway, Oakwood Press, 2001
   (Revised Edition, 2007)
The Coniston Railway, Oakwood Press, 2007
The Kendal & Windermere Railway, Oakwood Press, 2012
The Mansfield-Southwell-Rolleston Railway, Oakwood Press, 2021

Front cover: Gresley 'K3/2' class 2-6-0 No. 61914 leaves Mansfield with a return excursion train from Skegness bound for Kirkby-in-Ashfield on 14th June, 1958.
J. Cupit

Author's note

   An article written by me on the Mansfield Railway appeared in the August 1976 edition of *Railway World*. Thereafter I carried out a great deal of further research in order to create the manuscript for a book. This work has been ongoing since then but has been interspersed with the research done for the five titles relating to my books on lines in the Lake District.
   Many of the people who gave me assistance, not least Eric Brailsford, who witnessed the opening ceremony of the Mansfield Railway, have died since the work began but I record my thanks to them in an appropriate place.
   The lines in Cumbria attract a lot of interest, not least because of the area in which they are or were located. It has therefore been gratifying to realize that what I had thought might only be a railway of my own childhood memories, still holds a great deal of interest for a lot of people.

Oakwood Press, 54-58 Mill Square, Catrine, KA5 6RD
Tel: 01290 551122 *Website:* www.stenlake.co.uk

Contents

	Prologue	5
Chapter One	**Why build this railway?**	
	The Nottinghamshire and Derbyshire coalfields – Moving the coal – The various companies – Mining moves eastwards – The need to serve new collieries – Efforts to bring better rail communications to Mansfield and district – The railway nobody wanted to build – A local group takes the initiative and a scheme is drawn up – 'The Mansfield Railway'	7
Chapter Two	**The scheme gets underway, 1910-1917**	
	The Bill and Act – The railway opens in three stages initially for freight – Mansfield Colliery to Clipstone, with an opening ceremony – Mansfield to Mansfield Colliery – Kirkby to Mansfield – The army camp at Clipstone – The inspection and approval to carry passengers	16
Chapter Three	**Another opening ceremony, 1917-1923**	
	Passenger trains begin – The first GCR timetable – Progress and consolidation – The company takes over the Concentration Sidings – The Rufford branch is opened – Further plans and another Bill – Blidworth and Bilsthorpe considered – Holidays and excursions	53
Chapter Four	**The LNER era, 1923-1947**	
	The coalfield expands – The Blidworth branch – The Bilsthorpe branch – The Mid-Notts Railway – J.P. Houfton – The completed line described – The period up to nationalization – The working timetable for 1927 when the line was at its zenith – A wrong working – World War II – Snow – The post-war period – The end of an era	75

Chapter Five	**Nationalization, 1948 and beyond**	
	Nationalization of the coal industry and the railway system – British Railways – The 1950 accident – The 'Fast Fish' – 1955: Final passenger services – Excursion trains after World War II until closure – 1966: A special excursion – The closure of the line to the west of Mansfield Colliery – The line continues to serve the collieries – The national miners' strike and the aftermath – The collieries are closed and the line becomes all but redundant	101
Chapter Six	**Motive power**	143
Chapter Seven	**Some recollections of the line**	153
	Postscript	154
Appendix One	**Acts of Parliament**	155
Appendix Two	**Opening sequence**	155
Appendix Three	**Langwith Junction and Shirebrook shed allocations**	157
Appendix Four	**The collieries served by the railway**	158
	Sources, locations and thanks	159
	Index	160

Prologue

'Old King Coal is supreme. He has no serious challenger and there is no threat to his reign'. Words spoken at a miners' gala held in Nottinghamshire in the late 1940s. Coal had become established as the fuel meeting the major part of Britain's energy requirements, from massive power stations to domestic fire grates. Moving that coal became, to a great extent, the responsibility of the railways and one such attendant was the Mansfield Railway. Yet this railway, once built, had a much wider use. The legendary 'fast fish' trains coming from Grimsby and Hull with their perishable loads for distribution across the Midlands and further south used this line. Through express trains from Leeds to Nottingham with through coaches for Bournemouth also used the line, calling at Mansfield, and a restaurant car express ran from Mansfield to London Marylebone. During World War I the railway served the large army camp near Forest Town. After World War II it was used extensively to take the families of this mining area to holiday or take a day excursion on the East Coast and further.

And yet, ultimately, when all else had gone, it became exclusively the courtier of the mighty monarch which had brought it into existence and was graced by his presence - but if ever that monarch should be dethroned …

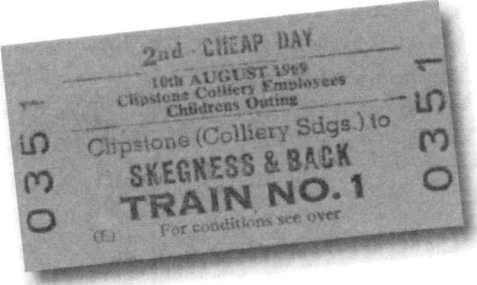 

The Mansfield Railway was planned and built much later than the Victorian period, when railway building was at its height, and schemes were often grand and ambitious. Times and attitudes had changed considerably. The motives, too, were, in many ways, different. Yet one aspect is to be found here which was found so often in the earlier sagas of the history of railway building but much less so in the later years, especially when it came to the smaller schemes; namely, a group of individuals, determined to achieve their objective and, if necessary, prepared to 'go it alone' to do so.

Often referred to simply as 'The Central' as opposed to 'The Midland' and with a station in Mansfield that stood on a road named 'Great Central Road' it was never owned by the Great Central Railway; only operated by that company. The Mansfield Railway remained an independent company down to the Grouping in 1923.

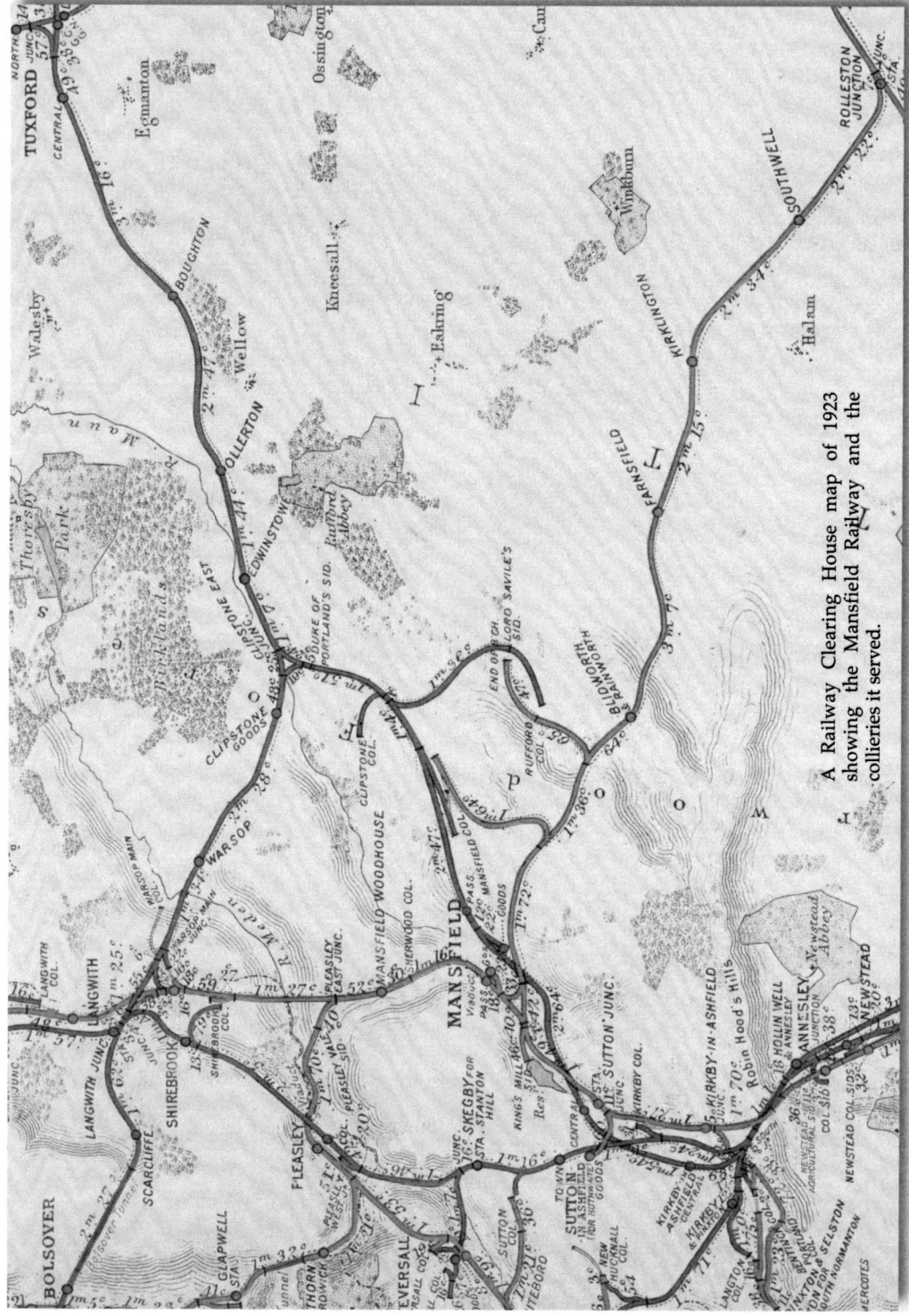

A Railway Clearing House map of 1923 showing the Mansfield Railway and the collieries it served.

Chapter One

Why build this railway?

There is no doubt that the industrial revolution, with its beginnings in the 18th century, gained momentum in the 19th century because coal became more readily available.

Initially, during this period, the facilities for the movement of coal were limited and when the demand became greater, it was the rivers (in this area, especially the River Trent) and, later, canals which provided a solution. In Derbyshire (and, initially, to a more limited extent, in Nottinghamshire) a network of canals was cut to move the coal; the Cromford, the Erewash, the Nutbrook, the Nottingham, along with others, each with its attendant tramways. The coalfield extending across Derbyshire and Nottinghamshire was to become one of the richest and most extensive in the country and it eventually became apparent that these two counties were by no means the limit of this field; it stretched further eastwards into Lincolnshire.

The second half of the 18th century saw a massive shift in methods for moving coal as canal transport gave way to rail transport. If coal was the life blood of the industrial revolution, the railways became the arteries along which that life blood was conveyed. The amount of coal being taken out of the Derbyshire and Nottinghamshire coalfields escalated. Trade was brisk. However, the coal in the east of Nottinghamshire lies deeper than that to the west and in Derbyshire and so more advanced techniques were required to mine it. In the early part of the 20th century such techniques were becoming available. The prospect for this area looked good. It became possible to develop larger and more sophisticated colliery workings. the financing of which would be justified by being able to mine coal at deeper levels. The result would be that these offered more in terms of output than the older and comparatively smaller collieries in the west. These new collieries would need to be served by railways and there were reasons to hope there would be competitive rates.

With a view to developing these deeper seams, once the technology was available, the Bolsover Colliery Co. sank a mine just to the east of Mansfield. This colliery was known simply as the Mansfield Colliery (or, locally, Crown Farm Colliery). When it opened in 1905, the Midland Railway, already the strongest player in the coalfield, was ready to serve it, using a branch, constructed in 1902, from its Mansfield-Southwell line. At this stage the Midland was the only railway in the vicinity. There were, however, misgivings about this monopoly for a number of reasons and even by this time there had been a long saga involving an aspiration to improve the provision of railway facilities in the district with Mansfield in particular in mind.

The railway nobody wanted to build

This saga began in 1865 with a proposal to build a railway from Mansfield to Retford. A Bill was prepared and came up for consideration by a Parliamentary select committee on 13th June, 1865. This Bill was opposed by the Midland Railway, the Duke of Portland, the Duke of Newcastle, the Manchester, Sheffield and Lincolnshire Railway (MS&LR), the Great Northern Railway (GNR) and a number of landowners along the route of the proposed line. The Parliamentary select committee heard evidence over a period of four days. The counsel for the promoters consisted of Mr Denison QC and Mr Gates. Messrs Toogood were the agents. The proceedings were very protracted. The Midland and the MS&LR both argued that they proposed to go to Mansfield. At one stage the view was expressed that there was, in fact, no coal under the line from Mansfield to Retford but this was later refuted! On 16th June it was announced that the preamble for the Bill was not found to be proved and therefore the scheme failed. This was not the last to be heard of these proceedings, however, as they were referred to again at a much later date. Matters seem to have rested there for 26 years. In 1891, Mansfield was incorporated as a municipal borough and moved, almost immediately, to seek better railway facilities for the town. With this in mind, a Railway Communications Committee (RCC) was set up. Over the next few years, this committee demonstrated a remarkable degree of persistence and determination to achieve the objective for which it was formed. The saga became a tortuous one.

First a resolution was passed asking the Directors of the GNR to receive a deputation with a view to making a railway connection for Mansfield. No response resulted from this. In February 1892, the Committee asked the Midland to provide better facilities but to no avail. The GNR was approached again and Henry Oakley (the General Manager of the GNR) did meet a deputation and asked for plans to be submitted. These plans, it seems, were not only virtually ignored, they were never returned! In the same month, similar deputations were made to the MS&LR and the Lancashire Derbyshire and East Coast Railway (LD&ECR). The correspondence with the RCC indicates that the MS&LR felt unable to act at that time; the LD&ECR Board did agree to consider the situation. In July 1892, there was a further resolution to ask the LD&ECR, once again, to receive a deputation and, further, in November of that year a deputation did meet with the Directors of the MS&LR. Events seemed to be moving in the right direction and plans were prepared by the borough surveyor. The route envisaged started at Annesley and went via Kirkby-in-Ashfield, Sutton-in-Ashfield, Mansfield, Mansfield Woodhouse, Clipstone, Ollerton and on to Retford. The Board of the MS&LR was asked to consider these proposals at its next meeting. The issue, however, became somewhat clouded by another proposal to construct a railway from Matlock to Kirkby. The RCC, not wishing to miss an opportunity, requested, on 4th May, 1893, that this proposed railway should extend to Mansfield. On 31st May, the London and North Western Railway (LNWR) was asked to work the line. No real progress followed and so in April 1894, the RCC decided to approach the LD&ECR again and the Directors were asked to consult with Thomas Turner, agent to the Duke of Portland, for his view. Once again there was no significant outcome. In May, the LNWR applied for powers to build a line from Northampton via Nottingham to Retford. Yet again the RCC asked for Mansfield to be included and, yet again, there was no affirming response. On 30th August, 1894, a public meeting was convened in connection with a proposed link with the LD&ECR. This meeting gave its backing to such a link and a petition was sent to the Directors.

In 1895 another alternative line was proposed, this time from Ashbourne, and the LNWR was approached but any possibility of involving Mansfield in the scheme was ruled out. The GNR was the next company to be re-petitioned by the RCC, this time for an extension to the Leen Valley Line from Kirkby to Pleasley and a connection to Mansfield was sought. The GNR declined to make such a connection. Undaunted, it seems, the RCC sent another deputation to the GNR in June 1895. As before, there was no progress. In July 1895 it was the turn of the MS&LR to be wooed again. Discussions were held but the MS&LR still had no real interest in a scheme. Similar unsuccessful deputations took place in 1896 and 1897. No company, it seemed, had any desire to provide a further link with Mansfield. The only one which did show some interest during the deliberations was the LD&ECR which had already listened to the wishes of the RCC with some sympathy. In 1896, it considered promoting an extension from its main line at Clipstone. However, the provision by the LD&ECR did not comply with the standing orders and so the Midland succeeded in blocking this proposal. Following this, it seems a deal was made whereby the LD&ECR was authorized to build a goods depot at Mansfield and then have running powers over the Midland. The goods depot was not built and the running powers never taken up. Later, after the LD&ECR had been absorbed into the Great Central Railway (GCR), this company tried to invoke this agreement for running powers. It was denied these by the Midland, whereupon it took the Midland to court in order to resolve the issue. The court upheld the position of the Midland when the case was heard in the Court of the First Instance so the GCR went to the Court of Appeal. The Midland still remained the victor; the GCR lost its appeal. It seems there were two grounds. The first was that running powers were provisional on the goods depot being built and it had not been. This matter would be referred to again later. The second, and seemingly stronger case, was that the running powers had been granted to the LD&ECR and were not automatically transferred with transfer of ownership.

In April 1898 the GNR was approached again but refused a request from the RCC for another deputation. During May, in what seemed a change of heart, it asked to be furnished with the proposals Mansfield Corporation had made and the borough surveyor submitted the plans. (Clearly, someone had forgotten it already had a copy!) The GNR failed to reply and in January 1899 it was asked whether the Directors were now ready to receive a deputation. There was still no response and in July the RCC pressed for a reply. The GNR simply reaffirmed that it did not believe the time was right to bring the Leen Valley to Mansfield and there was a suggestion that the £200,000 needed to build it would not be well spent given the probable level of traffic it might carry. By now, new collieries were being planned and in June 1901, with Sherwood Colliery, near

Mansfield, just opened, the GNR was petitioned again. In August the GNR made it clear that it would not receive a deputation but with sheer tenacity, in June 1902, the RCC sought once again to meet the company. The RCC again pressed for a response when the Board of the GNR failed to reply but then it seemed for a moment that the importunity of the RCC had paid off. The GNR conceded it would work the line if it was locally built. Mansfield town council, possibly in a state of minor euphoria, immediately offered £250 towards promoting the scheme. This scheme would, if realized, include Sherwood Colliery and discussions followed between the owners of the colliery and the GNR. The council's hopes were dashed when, for no apparent reason, the GNR announced that it could not work the line even if it were to be built. The situation was back to the proverbial 'square one'.

At this stage another very significant factor came into play which resulted in further moves being made during the early 1900s. The colliery owners, in particular the Bolsover Colliery Company, which was responsible for operating Mansfield Colliery, began to take an active interest. In 1906, a group approached both the GNR and GCR with a proposal to resurrect the plan to make a line from Annesley but this time to take it to Clipstone. Other considerations were coming to the fore. It was pointed out that such a line would significantly reduce the distance by rail between Grimsby and London but still neither company showed any interest. In 1909 the group, including some of the colliery owners, wined and dined the representatives of the GNR at the Swan Inn in Mansfield, well known for its high culinary standards. The meeting was relaxed and amicable. It was also informal in the sense that no minutes were taken. It soon became clear that the way to the GNR Directors' hearts (or railway) was not through their stomachs; the meeting produced no further action.

By this time the Bolsover Colliery Company was getting desperate, needing, as it did, to move coal more effectively, especially to the ports on the East Coast. There was still no help in sight and so the colliery company decided to pursue the possibility of building a private mineral line from Mansfield Colliery to Clipstone. This scheme, too, proved impossible to realize. It was opposed, and formidably so, by the Duke of Portland who was adamant that his estate would not be used in this way. He owned land over which some seven of the ten miles of the railway would pass and therefore without his co-operation the project was a lost cause. The Duke, however, threw out something of a life-line and possibly sowed the seeds that would geminate into a later plan; he pointed out that if the line was a 'public line' he would support it. His stance seemed to give weight to the notion that what was needed, if a line was to be built, was a new company to do the building.

A scheme to challenge the Midland

The outcome was that at this point the group made a decision to advance the cause of providing Mansfield with a second railway, creating competition for the Midland and serving the developing coalfield. Like similar groups had done in the past in similar circumstances, it was agreed that if a line was to be constructed, the best solution was for them to make provision to build it. Without approaching anyone else at this juncture, it was resolved to form a company; namely the Mansfield Railway Company. This consisted to a large extent, and perhaps not surprisingly, of colliery people. One of the leading figures was J.Plowright Houfton, the Managing Director of the Bolsover Colliery Company. (He was joined later by R.M. Knowles, Chairman of the same company). W.J. Chadburn, a managing partner of the Mansfield Brewery was also in the group, which further included Emerson Bainbridge. The latter (his full name was Emerson Muschamp Bainbridge) was a man of some consequence. A mining engineer from Sheffield, he had founded the Bolsover Colliery Co. and later became closely associated with the scheme to build the LD&ECR. He joined the Board of the LD&ECR in 1892 and, eventually, was Chairman for a time. Mansfield Corporation was only too willing to support the plan. At a meeting on 19th November, 1909 a resolution was passed unanimously that 'The Town Council, having had the scheme for the proposed line connecting to the Great Central Railway at Kirkby with the Great Central Railway at Clipstone, via Mansfield explained by the promoters, welcome the proposals with great cordiality, express general approval of the scheme and promise to give every support in their power'.

The Select Committee deliberates

A Bill was drawn up by Davies, Sanders and Swanwick, solicitors in Chesterfield, and in conjunction with W. and W.M. Bell, Parliamentary Agents of Dean's Yard, Westminster, was submitted without delay. It is dated 16th November, 1909. The line planned would leave the GCR at Kirkby-in-Ashfield and go via Sutton-in-Ashfield and Mansfield to Clipstone where it would rejoin the GCR on the former LD&ECR line. The original intention was to have a forked junction at Kirkby and this is shown on the plans submitted with the Bill. However, in the initial stages the Mansfield Railway Company asked for this proposal to be deleted from the Bill and only the plan for a south-facing junction to be retained. The reason not to proceed with the northern fork seems to have been an awareness that the only landowner ready to object to the Bill, the Hodgkinson Trust, owned land in this area. The trustees, in particular Catherine Anne Hodgkinson and Thomas Clarke Hodgkinson, acting for the (Mary Ann) Hodgkinson Trust were preparing to mount a vigorous opposition to the plans because the land it owned had already been 'violated' (their word) by other railways in the area cutting across it and the fork would have the effect of slicing a section of the Trust's remaining land into three parcels. The Mansfield Railway Co., in seeking to abandon this element of the Bill, put forward its own reason, possibly to save face to some extent. It would be argued at the Parliamentary committee stage that the northerly fork was impracticable 'given the terrain and that there is a deep declivity'. In the Bill there were four sections.

Railway No. 1 which included the southerly fork and extended to the Mansfield boundary.
Railway No. 2 which went on from here to a point just east of Mansfield.
Railway No. 3 continued from here and went on to form the eastern curve onto the GCR at Clipstone.
Railway No. 4 consisted of the northerly fork at Kirkby-in-Ashfield which the Mansfield Railway sought to abandon.

The House of Lords select committee began its deliberations on Tuesday 5th April, 1910. The chairman was the Duke of Wellington. Putting the case for the proposers was Mr Honoratus Lloyd. The deliberations would take four days. Honoratus Lloyd was an eloquent and convincing proponent. He began by pointing out that 'the Bill is a proposal on behalf of many local gentlemen of considerable position and wealth who desire to see the district in which they are deeply interested supplied with further railway facilities'. He lamented the fact that 'the Bill is one of the few illustrations of private enterprise that will come before Parliament this session'. He went on to describe how Mansfield was not only important for coal but for 'motor carriage works, iron foundries, engineering works, boot factories, hosiery and other factories'. He made clear the problems associated with getting coal from the Mansfield Colliery to the ports on Humberside; the congestion at the [Mansfield] colliery with only one service line and the circuitous route needed to get to Humberside; of the aspiration of Mansfield Corporation that the LD&ECR would help out and the 'fact' that in his view 'there has been something of the nature of an unholy alliance between the railways themselves to feather their own nests and keep the district without further railway communication'. He outlined the proposals of 1896 and the numerous unsuccessful attempts to interest a company in providing another railway facility for Mansfield. He went on to describe the coming of the new colliery developments and the need to move not only the coal which was being produced but also the greater amounts that would be produced.

There was a minor altercation at this stage when he raised the matter of the proposed Mansfield goods depot and the running powers with which it had been linked. Some did not accept this and felt the key issue in denying running powers was the result of a change of company (from LD&ECR to GCR). Turning to the matter of the northerly fork, Honoratus Lloyd asked the members of the select committee to ignore this proposal when making their decision. Members of the select committee were then informed that the GCR had provisionally agreed to work the line. Although the Hodgkinson Trust raised objections to the scheme the main opponent was seen as the Midland. Honoratus Lloyd informed the select committee: 'They [The Midland] have been around for sixty years enjoying a monopoly and they hope to persuade you [the select committee] to let them keep it!'

The Midland case was put by Mr Talbot. He referred back to the proposed Mansfield and Retford Railway of 1865. The Midland suggested there had been an agreement that if the Mansfield and Retford was abandoned the Midland would grant running powers to the LD&ECR between Mansfield and Worksop. 'So why had these not been taken up?' This argument seemed to gain little credence.

A number of worthies were called to give evidence. The first was Plowright Houfton, then Emerson Bainbridge followed by William Chadburn (who recounted how he had petitioned the LNWR for a railway facility to provide a better route for hops, barley and timber; all needed for The Mansfield Brewery, of which he was a Director); Frederick Johnson (who owned mills in the district); Timothy Taylor (a grocer); Henry Collins (the Mayor of Mansfield and a member of the Railway Communications Committee); John Harrop White (the Town Clerk, who gave very lengthy evidence which detailed the events leading up to the formation of the Mansfield Railway Company); Albert Ball (the Mayor of Nottingham); Edward Alcock (an alderman); Thomas Turner (for The Duke of Portland); and William Carter (President of the Nottinghamshire Miners Association).

On the following day, 6th April Mr Talbot presented a lengthy case on behalf of the Midland during which he raised a few eyebrows by asserting that the Midland did not consider it had a monopoly in the area because other companies (the GCR was mentioned) were operating to considerable effect.

Sam Fay gives evidence

On the same day Sam Fay (the General Manager of the GCR) was called to give evidence relating to matters regarding the GCR and its dealings with the proposed Mansfield Railway. In response to questions put by Mr Macassey, acting for the promoters, Fay acknowledged that his company had, in the past, been pressed to construct a link to Mansfield and pointed out that financial constraints had not permitted the advancing of such a project. He felt that the scheme under consideration was a sound one and the GCR would be ready to work the railway, not least because a new, extensive dock was under construction at Immingham and the Mansfield Railway would be an important link in providing an outlet from this. There was also the additional facility the Mansfield Railway would provide in moving coal from Mansfield Colliery. Fay made it clear that the GCR was not promoting the Mansfield Railway but it was simply dealing with a proposal to work the line. There had, he conceded, been an approach to work a branch from the line at Clipstone to the Mansfield Colliery but then the group involved in this scheme had come up with a more comprehensive project; namely the one under consideration.

Responding to Mr Talbot, Fay, when under cross-examination, said he was unable to comment on the proceedings in 1865 as he had no documentation. Talbot then produced an Act of Parliament and this seemed to give rise to some mild confusion as Fay, whilst expressing an interest was clearly unable to respond to the questions. What Talbot was leading up to was the fact that the GCR had running powers over the Midland. Fay replied that he was aware of the situation whereby the GCR, under a reciprocal agreement with the Midland, had running powers into Mansfield but that he had not been involved in correspondence regarding congestion at Mansfield station (it had involved Mr Wilmott, the then manager of the LD&ECR) but that four years previously the GCR had ceased working passenger services from Sheffield to Mansfield via

Worksop because it was unremunerative. Fay went on to inform the committee, after further questioning by Talbot (who had suggested that in working the new line what the GCR would, in effect, be doing was transferring the traffic from its own line and putting it onto the new line) that in his view there would be no loss in receipts because the new line was a better route. Talbot then changed tack. He questioned Fay about the possibility of a through train from Mansfield to London. Talbot pressed Fay hard on this one:

Talbot	Now witnesses from Mansfield talked a great deal about a through passenger service to London and they greatly complained that they had to change carriages at Nottingham by Midland.
Fay	Yes.
Talbot	Have you undertaken to provide a through service from Mansfield to London without changing?
Fay	No, we have made no arrangement whatsoever with the promoters except to say that we are prepared to work it at 60% of the receipts.
Talbot	Will you undertake to do what I put to you in regard of that?
Fay	I think so.
Talbot	Will you undertake to give a through service from Mansfield to London?
Fay	Yes, I think so.
Talbot	Will you undertake that?
Fay	Yes, I think so. We are already running by a circuitous route between Lincoln and London via Chesterfield, one train in the morning and one in the afternoon. That would naturally be transferred to this route because it would serve Mansfield as well.
Talbot	Are you prepared to undertake before Parliament or to put into the Bill the obligation to run a bona fide through service for passengers from Mansfield to London?
Fay	Yes.

Next Mr Clode questioned Fay on behalf of the GNR.

During this short session Fay made some interesting comments saying that the GCR and GNR were 'practically as one' and that they were 'brothers in arms'. (This comment may possibly have been based on the fact that in November 1907, the GNR and GCR had reached 'heads of agreement' regarding co-operation and the sharing of receipts but progress was stalled because the Railway and Canal Commission Court rejected these. In spite of this the co-operation continued and the Great Eastern Railway also joined the group. Following this a 'three companies Bill' was deposited for the 1909 session which, if successful, would, in effect, have lead to an amalgamation. The passage of this Bill seemed set to go through but then a number of protective clauses were added which took out many of the anticipated advantages. The Bill was withdrawn although some co-operation did continue.)

There was another short altercation at this point between Talbot and Clode regarding who was entitled to ask questions about what, in relation to the Act cited previously and which Clode wanted to use. Macassey, for the promoters, intervened and said he assumed there had been the intention to show that the

GCR was not in a position to make an agreement with the Mansfield company but in his view this had not been done. Under Macassey there was further questioning regarding routes and basically he aimed to establish that the liaison between the GCR and Mansfield Railway would bring considerable benefits. Finally the Chairman put his own questions relating to the suggestion by the GNR that the new line should stop at the junction with the GNR and whether this might cause problems with traffic on the GNR. Fay seemed rather ambivalent about this and at this point the session finished.

The Bill goes forward and becomes an Act

The select committee proceedings continued until 8th April when, after considering the evidence, it decided for the proposers, so enabling their Bill to go forward. The resulting Act is dated 26th July, 1910.

So it was that the Mansfield Railway came to be built. Late in the period usually associated with private railway construction and yet, in some ways remarkably, it did (or, more realistically, had to) begin as an independent company. What is more, it was to remain one of the small group of lines holding on to independence until the amalgamation of 1921-23 which gave rise to just four railway companies. At this stage the Mansfield Railway would be absorbed into the London & North Eastern Railway (the LNER).

This photograph was taken before the building of the railway commenced, showing the popular area called 'The Meadows' (later Titchfield Park) adjacent to Nottingham Road in Mansfield. The buildings in the background were demolished to make way for an embankment to carry the railway. *Eric Brailsford*

Chapter Two

The scheme gets underway, 1910-1917

1910

On the 27th July, 1910, the day following the placing of the Act on the Statute Book, the Directors, Messrs Bainbridge, Houfton and Chadburn with H.Sanders 'in attendance', met at the Royal Victoria Hotel in Sheffield. Houfton was appointed Chairman. The main item on the agenda for discussion at the meeting was the formalizing of an agreement with the GCR. This included (i) a working agreement (ii) an agreement as to traffic (iii) the rates for this and (iv) a purchase agreement. The second and third items had also previously been approved by the Bolsover Colliery Company. The Board resolved that the company seal should be fixed to all the financial arrangements. It was agreed that negotiations with the GNR should be continued. The solicitors' report on Contract No. 1 was adopted and in reference to the Parliamentary deposit, the solicitors reported that £752 5*s*. 0*d*. would be released by the abandonment of Railway No. 4. The meeting was concluded with Sanders being appointed the Secretary and authorized to obtain a seal.

Robert Elliott-Cooper would be the Engineer. He had, like a number of others involved in the project, been associated with the LD&ECR, having been Engineer for that line.

On 28th October the Agreement was signed between the Mansfield Railway Company and the GCR. The document runs into 16 detailed clauses and the overall impression given is that the GCR will be firmly in control. For example at one point it is stipulated that if the GCR at any time after the completion of the line found it necessary to purchase further land for sidings or buildings of any sort ('station agents' houses, sheds, warehouses' are included) then the cost would be met by the Mansfield Company. There was a caveat attached to this that if the Mansfield Railway failed to carry out such works and the GCR found it had to do so, all costs involved would be passed to the Mansfield Railway. In another clause the GCR also stated that it would have the rights to fix the rates for through and local traffic.

The next Agreement was signed the following day, 29th October. This one involved the Mansfield Railway, the GCR and the Bolsover Colliery Co. It reiterated what had been agreed in the previous document using the 'Whereas' clause and by this short document the Bolsover Colliery Co. agrees to procure the land necessary for building all the sidings it will need including those required for the storage of wagons. The Bolsover company gives an undertaking that once the Mansfield and Rufford Collieries are open it will guarantee that not less than 500,000 tons of coal per annum will be sent by way of the Mansfield Railway and the GCR.

In a third Agreement dated the 31st October, also between the three companies, the previous agreement is ratified and there is an additional clause in which the Bolsover company will get a reduction in rates by the Mansfield

Company and GCR when compared to others rates, of sixpence per ton for coal carried to Grimsby and Immingham and a halfpenny per ton for coal being taken in the opposite direction, to Kirkby-in-Ashfield and beyond.

On 9th December, a second meeting was held at the Royal Victoria Hotel in Sheffield. The original members were joined by A.S. Wills, who at this stage was anticipating his company would build the line. It was announced that agreements had been exchanged with the GCR and it was hoped these would have been in place by 28th October that year, although confirmation by the Railway and Canal Commissioners was awaited. Discussion ensued regarding the section of work from Mansfield Colliery to Clipstone and it was agreed to ascertain the views of the Duke of Portland. Wills intimated that his firm was ready to start construction. It turned out that he was rather premature in his assumptions.

In the meantime Haig Brown was asked to provide estimates for annual traffic revenues and he submitted this in a report dated 7th November.

The figures he produced were broken down into considerable detail but in principle the income from mineral traffic, which in fact was entirely coal, amounted to £22,416 8s. 0d.

(There is an interesting reference in the listings to the proposed sinking of The King Edward VII Pit. Edward had died the previous May and was well known for his love of the Dukeries and frequent visits there but this proposal to name a colliery in his memory would seem to have been abandoned.)

For the revenue from passenger traffic, Haig Brown put in total at £14,904 16s. 9d. and this figure, again, is broken down into sections. These include what he describes as 'ordinary passenger traffic' (by which he means traffic arising from or terminating at Mansfield line stations), excursion traffic (based from stations on the Mansfield line) and through passenger and excursion traffic. He also adds the revenue from 'Paddy Trains', these being for the transport of colliers.

He then lists an estimate totalling £7,568 for general goods and finally £6,000 for traffic such as parcels and mail with a separate section for the fish traffic which would pass over the line. He points out that no estimates have been included for the possible transporting of livestock.

The total revenue he estimated would be in the order of £50,888 but these figures would be revised a number of times over the next seven years with a figure of £41,641 at one stage and by 1917, a total of £50,898.

1911

The next meeting took place on 11th February, 1911. Information about the allocation of the £125,000 ordinary shares was given. The Bolsover Colliery Co., £62,500, C.J. Wills & Sons, £16,000, R. Elliott-Cooper, £5,000, M. Attwood, £7,500 and Timothy Taylor, £1,000. There were also proposals for Bainbridge, £5,000, Houfton, £2,000 and Chadburn, £2,000. The hope was expressed that the Duke of Portland would subscribe. It was resolved that Chadburn and Houfton would form a committee to deal with the Prospectus, capital and the allotment of shares. The bankers would be the Union of London & Smiths Bank Ltd (at the Mansfield branch) and an account was to be opened immediately. Additional

Directors were appointed and both were already Directors of other railway companies. They were Thomas Craven of Kirklington Hall, near Southwell, a Director of the Cambrian Railway, and Samuel Wilkinson Pilling of Welton Hall, Brough, Yorkshire, a Director of the Wrexham & Ellesmere Railway. The plans were progressing well and there was a good deal of satisfaction.

An EGM was held on 2nd March, 1911, to discuss in more detail the agreement with the GCR and on this occasion the meeting took place in Chesterfield. Concern was aired about the problems which might arise for shareholders if the company was ever sold to the GCR. The Bolsover Colliery Co. seemed to take a keen interest in this aspect. Fears were allayed but in the event it was not a problem which ever had to be faced. In March, Frank Cook was appointed the land valuer and surveyor by the Board when it met in Sheffield on 29th March, 1911, although his brief did not include land to be acquired from the Duke of Portland and the Hodgkinson Trustees. Robert Anderson was assigned this element and also to deal with tenant rights. At this meeting a draft Prospectus was considered and also Wills' tender for the work. However, at this point some reservations were expressed. It is not altogether clear why but it may be that there were those who felt only one horse in the race hardly made it a race! The outcome was that Elliott-Cooper was asked to prepare a report so that comparisons might be made. Further there was a feeling that the GCR should be consulted in case there was a public tender. More shares had been allocated; a total of 548 in all and the good news was that the Duke of Portland had taken 10,000 ordinary shares, 5,000 5 per cent preference shares and 5,000 in debenture stock; this being subject to the whole line being constructed. At a special meeting on the same day, preference shares to the value of £125,000 were created carrying a preferential dividend of 5 per cent, together with a premium if the GCR bought to an amount not exceeding 25 per cent of the nominal value of these preference shares.

Bainbridge, Elliott-Cooper and Sanders met in an auspicious venue, the Royal Courts of Justice, on 5th May, 1911. The purpose was to consider the final draft of the Prospectus and this was approved and signed. The company's brokers, Lawson and Ormerod had advised this should be advertised on 13th May and the lists opened on 15th May and closed on 17th May. In fact the Prospectus is dated 17th May and the lists are given as opening on 22nd May and closing on 24th May. The capital to be raised was £250,000 by 12,500 5 per cent preference shares of £10 each, 12,500 ordinary shares at £10 each, an issue of 12,500 preference shares at £10 each and 11,000 ordinary shares at £10 each, at par. A deposit of 10s. per share was required on application with £1 10s. on allotment. The 'Object of the Railway', which is described as being promoted by 'the citizens of Mansfield, the Bolsover Colliery Co. and other influential traders' [interestingly, in that order] is 'to obtain for Mansfield new railway facilities to place the town upon a through main line between London and Grimsby and Immingham'. It points out that Mansfield, a town with a population of 70,000, has only one railway, the Midland. It further points out that following the Special Act of 28th October, 1910, the GCR will work and maintain the line at 60 per cent of its gross receipts. The Bolsover Colliery Co. had guaranteed 500,000 tons of coal per annum from its Mansfield and Rufford pits, by an agreement dated 29th October, 1910. Already Mansfield Colliery had an output of over one and a half million tons of coal per annum and it was estimated that Rufford, which was just about to be sunk, would produce 750,000 tons per annum. The Prospectus also referred to the fact that passenger services would be an important element. A large local traffic was anticipated; the Midland was running 19 trains each way each weekday between Mansfield and Nottingham and five extra on Saturdays. In addition, the new line would form part of a main route to London as well as Leicester and Lincoln. The promoters were confident that the section between Mansfield Colliery and Clipstone would be ready within a year. It was agreed that 10,000 copies of a hand map should be produced. On another front, the matter of Wills' tender was considered again and it was decided to ask Sam Fay, of the GCR, to look at it and make any comments he felt appropriate. There had been an agreement to issue £110,000 of ordinary shares and there had already been 502 applications.

When the Directors met on 19th May they had suffered a blow. The man of influence, Emerson Bainbridge, had died on 12th May. The Board sent sympathy and condolences to his widow and family. The Prospectus was viewed and a list of newspapers drawn up where it would be advertised on 20th May. A special advertisement was approved for *The Times* newspaper on condition the cost did not exceed £50. Although Sanders had been acting as solicitor for the company, his position had not been formally confirmed and at the meeting his firm of Davies, Sanders and Swanwick was appointed. The Engineer's appointment was also formally approved. It was resolved that a call of 38s. per share on the 1,500 shares already allocated should be made. The matter of a replacement for Emerson Bainbridge was considered and it was felt Bertram Abel Smith of the London and Smiths Bank should be asked to fill the vacancy. The appointment was confirmed at the following meeting which took place on 26th May, in Sheffield. Another Director came on to the Board in the person of Robert Knowles, of Colston Bassett Hall near Bingham. Knowles, as mentioned, was a member of the Bolsover Colliery Company Board. Approval was given to the list of applicants for 11,000 shares at £10 each and those on a list for preference shares totalling £7,847. The Chairman and Pilling agreed to meet the Engineer to agree terms. Regret was expressed that Sam Fay had not come back to the Board with his observations on Wills' tender and so the Directors, having the view that time was of the essence, decided to go to public tender anyway. The result was that tenders for the works were available for consideration at the next Board meeting at the Station Hotel, Chesterfield on 29th June, 1911. They ranged from £145,629 15s. to £249,012 15s. 11d. It was decided that the eight lowest should be sent to the Engineer for consideration at a special meeting on 7th July at 15 Deans Yard, Westminster. In the meantime, it was agreed the Engineer should be paid £5 per cent upon the total cost of the works, excluding land remuneration but to include the drawings, plans and associated items.

By this time the company felt it was in a position to exercise its compulsory purchase powers and the solicitors were instructed to serve the orders. Consideration was also given to a ceremony for cutting the first sod and it was hoped the Duke of Portland would accept an invitation to do this. The Duke's agent had been approached and a reply was awaited. A shareholders' half-yearly meeting was planned for Tuesday 15th August at noon, in Sheffield. At the special meeting held on 7th July, it was decided that the tender submitted by Baldry, Yerburgh and Hutchinson for £147,411 18s. 10d. should, subject to finalizing details, be accepted. In view of this step, a works committee was appointed and the members of this were Messrs Houfton, Pilling, Craven and Knowles. (Baldry and Yerburgh had previously won the contract to build the Warsop to Tuxford section of the LD&ECR.) Quite what had happened behind the scenes remains a mystery but the Board suddenly decided that a ceremony for cutting the first sod was not appropriate and the plan was cancelled.

On 31st July there was a meeting of the committee appointed to deal with the contract for the works and this was held at the Station Hotel in Chesterfield. Baldry, Yerburgh and Hutchinson asked to be released from the condition involving sureties and in view of their previous experience this was agreed, although there was a condition that plant to the value of £30,000 should be put on the site and kept there. On the same day, the finance committee met at the same venue. The members were told that there were ample means to meet the existing financial demands and so a further call could be deferred. On 15th August there was a meeting at the Royal Victoria Station Hotel in Sheffield. The Board spent a considerable amount of time, as, indeed, it was to do in many subsequent meetings, discussing land purchase. This became a protracted business in some cases, with much effort spent in resolving problems associated with some of the lots. A substantial parcel of land belonged to the Duke of Portland and £5,000 had to be deposited to gain possession of this. Other plots needed immediately included land belonging to Brunts Charity, Winfield and 'others', Mansfield Brewery, Annie Burt and Kate Lewis. In addition a plot belonging to the Mansfield Church Estate was required. An easement from the GNR was needed at Kirkby-in-Ashfield. The matter of the possible purchase of Mansfield vicarage was discussed and it was decided this would probably have to be purchased, the price to be between £2,000 and £3,000. The works committee was asked to view the property and report back. Later Sam Fay would take an interest when the property had been purchased and, in the event, was not needed.

At the first half-yearly meeting of the shareholders, on the same day and at the same venue, the matter of the Directors' remuneration was raised and it was agreed £1,000 should be allocated in total to be divided up as they saw fit. This figure would not include expenses! Later, at a meeting of the finance committee held at the Swan Hotel on 17th October, it was agreed that the Chairman would receive £100 per annum and the other six Directors would share £450 equally between them. The remaining £450 was to be divided between the Directors in accordance with their attendances at Board and committee meetings, provided the latter were not held on Board days. Houfton and Craven were re-elected Chairman and Vice-Chairman respectively, roles they were to retain until the company was absorbed into the LNER in 1923. In the following months the company pressed ahead with the acquisition of land. As mentioned previously, a great deal of time was spent resolving issues of cost as claims were made which the company felt were too high. In general, agreements were reached but not in every case and problems were to arise which would hold up progress. Tenders were sought for rails and those received included £6 10s. per ton for ordinary 85 pound rails or 7s. 6d. per ton more for Sandberg steel rails. The GCR offered to provide the latter for £6 2s. 6d. per ton and this offer was accepted. What the company did not appear to realize was that these were 'second-hand' rails and this disclosure caused some consternation later!

The Directors also met on 17th October. Land possession was high on the agenda and involved the Mansfield Brewery, the Mansfield Grammar School, Mansfield Corporation and the Mansfield Church Charity. The Board gave an undertaking to pay interest at the rate of 5 per cent from the date of possession until the completion of purchase. Robert Anderson, for the Mansfield Railway Co., had agreed with the Bolsover Colliery Co. terms for the land needed by the railway which included their offices at the Mansfield Colliery. Further notices had been served in relation to land. One person on the list was Colonel Lindley who did not seem at all happy with the prospect of losing land to the railway. The Directors were informed of the progress that had been made; fairly basic at this time. About 1,782 yards of fencing had been completed with another 1,570 delivered and 6,170 cubic yards of soil had been excavated. There had been slow progress with work between the colliery and the main line and the hope was expressed that there would be as little delay as possible in future. A temporary line was being constructed in Section 1 of the contract, between Sheepbridge Lane and Nottingham Road to facilitate the construction of the bridges. The engineering questions associated with the construction of a bridge under the Midland company's Southwell line had been settled with that company and much of the preliminary work had been done. In general it was hoped the pace of the work would increase. Colonel Lindley did not submit a claim in relation to his land and, further, declined possession of his land on the usual terms. The Board, meeting on 14th November, 1911, expressed some consternation at this and decided to ask the Board of Trade to appoint a surveyor to fix the terms. The Engineer was particularly keen that this action should be taken quickly as he needed the land 'immediately'.

Colonel Lindley was not alone in holding up the proceedings. William Hollins was taking the same stance and so it was resolved similar action must be taken in his case. There was also something of a wrangle going on with Mansfield Corporation over the site of the old pumping station which was obsolete and disused. The Corporation put in a heavy claim on the grounds that the station might at some time be useful for subsidiary purposes, although these were not stated. Another matter needing careful consideration was the purchase of the vicarage land for the purpose of making an extension to Mansfield station. The GCR had approved of this but the Board was not at all convinced that the price was right and deferred a decision. Other land plots were acquired and Section 2 of the scheme saw satisfactory progress with some 50,000 cubic yards excavated and sidings laid down for full wagons for 'down' traffic. Work on the 'up' sidings was in hand, culverts were being made but bridges had yet to be started. Gone were the days, however, which saw blood, sweat and possibly tears, as gangs of navvies laboured with spades and barrows and possibly assisted by horses, to shift the tons of soil needed for the earthworks. By the beginning of the 20th century construction techniques had moved on considerably and the equipment list included eight locomotives (increasing eventually to 20, mainly 0-4-0 and 0-6-0 saddle tanks), three steam navvies, steam pumps, saw mills and a steam hammer.

Only 270 men were employed and this figure was to diminish with the onset of war. Eight and a half miles of temporary track were planned together with 17 temporary buildings.

Yet, in spite of all this, there was very little progress on Section 1, with the exception of the bridge under the Midland Railway. The lack of progress was down to Colonel Lindley who was refusing possession of a small strip of land required for crossing the occupation road leading to his quarry. The contractor was anxious to commence work on the bridges over the Nottingham Road and Littleworth and had started a temporary tramway to connect the site of these bridges with the quarry, from which the stone would be obtained. However, Colonel Lindley's advisors would not allow this temporary work to proceed. Hence there was no progress. In fact it had been possible, as mentioned, to progress the work on the bridge under the Midland line as bricks were used for the construction of this bridge. The matter of the GCR offer of rails came up again but the company decided not to take it up *pro tem as* there was uncertainty on the part of the Board about the wisdom of using second-hand rails. Further quotes were sought. There was good news on 14th November when Chadburn and Smith met in Nottingham at the Victoria Station Hotel. The surveyor for the Board of Trade had made his award in respect of Colonel Lindley and also William Hollins, fixing the amounts at £360 and £1,793 respectively. Action could now be taken and by 18th November it was possible to report that the lands in question had been acquired. In the meantime Mansfield Corporation had an axe to grind. The Board of Trade was contacted about the width of the bridge over Sherwood Hall Road. However, the Board of Trade pointed out that it had no power to intervene in this matter but did ask the company to send information on the circumstances. The company, a little aggravated by this, agreed to widen the bridge to 35 ft but with a proviso that the Corporation would agree to the diversion of Hermitage Lane and a reduction of the width of the bridge over the lane to 33 ft between the parapets.

In a letter, the vicar of Mansfield offered to sell the vicarage for £2,500 and the Board accepted this. The dilemma about new or second-hand rails was eventually referred to Sam Fay by the Secretary who was assured that used rails were quite in order. There had been a well established custom in 19th century railway building enterprises to ensure that the spiritual welfare of the navvies was catered for, through some arrangement with the Church, either by the company or, perhaps, a well-to-do person who lived in the locality where building was taking place. (When the Midland was being built through Mansfield, provision had been made for the spiritual well-being of the workers and a chapel was provided in Stockwell Gate, in Mansfield.) In this tradition, the Revd W.Tilley, the vicar of Saint John's church, in Mansfield, formed a committee with a responsibility to take up mission work amongst the navvies and he approached the Board to ask for financial support with this endeavour. Times had changed! The company did not feel able to help and suggested it might be more appropriate to approach the contractors. It was reported that there were no Bills to come before Parliament in 1912 which might pose a threat to the company and with a certain amount of satisfaction concerning the progress generally, the New Year started.

1912

The matter of rails was soon to find its way onto the agenda again and when the Board met on 12th January, it considered a letter from Sam Fay. The first reaction was that the cost was too high but later, on 16th February, there was a change of view and the price was agreed. However, when the Board met on 21st March, the members were informed that the GCR could not provide enough rails after all and so the company would have to look elsewhere! In January Bertram Abel Smith resigned, a move which the Board very much regretted. At the meeting in January, Houfton and Craven were re-elected as Chairman and Vice-Chairman. The wrangle continued with Mansfield Corporation over the pumping station, the corporation asking £5,550. In May the Directors were advised not to offer more that £3,500 although the surveyor felt £4,625 would not be unreasonable. The original cost for the station at Mansfield had been put at £12,397 5s. 2d. but this figure was revised upwards to £16,545 2s. 8d. and it was decided a new contract would be needed and so tenders were invited. Some consideration was given at this stage to the proposal to build a branch to Rufford Colliery but a decision was deferred. In the second week of June, Sam Fay was consulted about both the Rufford branch and the Clipstone branch but he felt no decision could be made until a proper costing had been carried out. The Board again decided to defer the whole matter.

One of the main topics to occupy the Directors' time throughout the year continued to be land acquisition. This included a substantial settlement with Barringer, Wallace & Manners (later The Metal Box Company) that had a factory to the east of Mansfield. The factory owners demanded £2,500 which the Board felt was too high. In October, the Board decided to seek further Parliamentary powers. These would include an extension of Kirkby Junction (involving a footpath diversion) extension of powers of purchase between Mansfield Colliery and Clipstone and permission to raise further capital. In addition it was agreed that the time had come to seek powers to construct the Clipstone and Rufford branches with another extension beyond to what was described as 'the new colliery to be sunk on Lord Savile's Estate', if the position could be defined clearly enough. Finally it was agreed that Parliamentary powers should be sought for a western curve to be made (onto the GCR line) at Clipstone. In order for coal traffic for Sheffield to reach Langwith it would be necessary for the locomotive to run round the train at Edwinstowe but a western curve would provide a through run to Warsop and beyond. (It is quite remarkable that this had not occurred to anyone at the outset!) The company's solicitor was given authority to act.

Throughout this period, work had been progressing on the construction of the line. There had been no incidents of note and any problems or set-backs although there were some problems of a different nature in the section between Kirkby-in-Ashfield and Sutton-in-Ashfield, namely the state of the terrain.

Eric Brailsford, who was alive when this account was written but sadly has since died, could remember the building of the line. He recalled 'From an early age I first heard the 'peep peep' of the little engines busy in what turned out to be the marshallling yard and of the one that brought the debris from the cutting being dug out from Sutton station to Kirkby–in–Ashfield. '

THE SCHEME GETS UNDERWAY, 1910-1917 25

This series of photographs show the type of machinery being used in the construction of the railway; a far cry from the many navvies and horses used in earlier days.
Courtesy Mansfield Museum with thanks to Liz Weston

The Directors decided, at the meeting in November, to inspect the section that had been constructed as soon as the works over Ratcliffe Gate, in Mansfield, would permit the passage of an engine and carriages. In December, the Board was informed there had been something of an obstacle as far as the Bill was concerned. Lord Savile and the Duke of Portland had both raised objections for powers to build the Rufford and Bilsthorpe branches. Further, the company's brokers advised against taking powers to raise further capital. Once again Sam Fay had been consulted and on 18th November he had strongly advised the Directors to abandon those parts of the Bill for the current session. As far as the footpath at Kirkby was concerned, it was hoped this problem could be resolved by asking the local authority to sanction a diversion. The Duke of Portland had said he would be happy to help in enabling the construction of the western curve and would facilitate this by selling land to the company by agreement. The Board accepted his offer.

During the initial discussions relating to the original Bill, the GNR had expressed an interest in running powers but did not accept a minimum toll of £2,000 per annum for this concession. No doubt feeling this had been a mistake, the company now came forward again with a decision that the £2,000 was acceptable. Circumstances, however, had changed and the Mansfield Railway Co. felt it could not give any undertaking without first consulting Sam Fay. As the year closed, the Directors agreed that a planned inspection of the line would take place on 12th December.

Work on the line progresses. *Courtesy Mansfield Museum with thanks to Liz Weston*

THE SCHEME GETS UNDERWAY, 1910-1917 27

1913

The beginning of 1913 saw a resolution of the matter relating to the waterworks and the company also agreed to pay £4,500 to widen Ratcliffe Gate. By March, the opening of the first portion of the line for mineral traffic was imminent and so a traffic advisor was sought who would agree a route table with the GCR. However, in April, the section from Mansfield and Clipstone was still not ready and the contractors were urged to complete it as soon as possible. A discussion was also held about the Concentration Sidings but any decisions were deferred until a meeting on 23rd May, when it was agreed that further approaches would have to be made to the Duke of Portland. Mr Haig-Brown, who, as was seen earlier, already had associations with the company, was appointed as traffic advisor. He was residing in Bournemouth at the time. He informed the Directors that coal traffic would commence between Mansfield and Clipstone on 16th June and the Secretary was asked to organize a ceremony for the occasion. One source indicates that the first train of coal to Immingham was as early as 6th June, although this is qualified by the statement 'regular traffic began ten days later'. Haig-Brown remained in the post of traffic advisor until 1922, although he narrowly escaped losing his position in 1920, when some Directors expressed the view that as the traffic situation had settled and rates had stabilized, he was no longer required. After discussion they decided he should be retained until 1921 but no further proposals were made to remove him and he was there when the company was taken into the LNER.

June 1913 – The first section is opened: Mansfield Colliery to Clipstone

The arrangements for the opening ceremony included a luncheon at the Swan Hotel in Mansfield. It is reported that 'the Directors of the new railway, colliery owners and managers, engineers and prominent local traders assembled at 1.30pm.' The luncheon was substantial 'served in Mr J.C. Ringham's well-known style.' (J.C. Ringham was the landlord of the Swan Hotel.) Houfton, who was also Mayor of Mansfield at the time, presided. Amongst those who sent apologies was Sam Fay. After the meal there came the usual round of speeches. Mr T.C. Higgins, for the GCR, proposed the health and prosperity of the railway, linking this toast closely with Houfton whom he felt could take much of the praise for what had been achieved. Higgins stated that he had every confidence that the railway would succeed. Houfton replied and in his speech made the rather surprising remark that no doubt Mr Higgins spoke 'feelingly' (we are told) for the Mansfield Railway because it was about the only thing that could bring salvation to the GCR! There are occasions when Houfton gave the marked impression that he did not care too much for the GCR; this was not the last but why he took this stance is not clear. (There has been speculation – and nothing more – that possibly Houfton had ordinary shares in the GCR. These did not pay a dividend and he hoped the Mansfield Railway would improve matters!) Another observation which Houfton offered concerned remarks he (Houfton) was alleged to have made in the past about Mansfield and which were perceived to be rather derogatory. In particular, some of the trades-people had been critical of what had been said but Houfton was adamant that these people had only themselves to blame because he wanted to make it clear that in his view Mansfield had a great future, not least because the coalfield would bring prosperity. He went on to outline the proposals for developing this coalfield and was very enthusiastic about the impact it would have on the economy of the area.

After this lengthy oration (Houfton went on to speak of matters involving Mansfield Town Council) a Mr Dermot spoke very briefly. He simply congratulated all involved in the scheme which he felt to be very sound. Finally Charles Markham, of Chesterfield, proposed a toast to the Chairman (Houfton) and sang his praises further. The party then left the Swan Hotel to carry out an inspection of the line between Mansfield Colliery and Clipstone. They went first to Pelham Street, where they boarded open trucks which had been fitted with improvised seats and were drawn by a contractor's locomotive. Apparently 'it was a boiling hot day, the warmest this summer and so the cool winds over the vast amount of forest was exceedingly grateful' [sic]. A number of people turned out to watch and at Mansfield Colliery the group stopped to see a coal train leave for Immingham. The contractor's engine reversed at Clipstone Junction and brought the party back to the Mansfield Colliery offices for refreshments 'after a short, sharp run'. A return trip was then made to Mansfield and the celebrations came to an end. There would be more junketing at a later date.

Moving on

Plans now moved further ahead to construct the rest of the line, namely the section from Mansfield to the existing section and then the final section from Kirkby-in-Ashfield. The purchase of land in the Kirkby area pressed ahead. Edward Hayes was among those who found they had to relinquish property as he gave over four houses and a plot of land for £1,050 (in spite of the fact that he had claimed £1,200). At the other end of the line attention turned again to the construction of the Concentration Sidings at Clipstone. Twenty-five acres of land would be needed with an additional 12 acres for severances. It was reckoned that this land would be needed as the traffic developed and £3,000 was proposed to include cover for tenant rights relating to the rearrangement and reconstruction of some farm buildings. The accommodation works, provided under the original agreement, had to be modified by the laying out of the sidings. The Duke of Portland decided to refer the whole matter to Alexander Ross, a former Engineer for the GNR, for advice and the claim for accommodation works was reduced to a bridge at just over three miles and a road at nine miles. It was felt the accommodation works would cause considerable interference with any future developments on the Concentration Sidings and the Duke of Portland intimated he would be willing to release the works on a payment of £4,000 and this was agreed. The Engineer, meanwhile, was given the authority to proceed with building Mansfield station, according to the plan, and shortly afterwards, in August, was instructed to start Mansfield goods yard. Tenders had been invited for signalling and the Railway Signal Co. was successful with a figure of £1,168 18s. 10d. It seemed that the GCR had agreed to meet the cost of installing the telegraph for £360 but later appeared to renege on this. However, the company informed the Mansfield Railway Company that it (the Mansfield Railway Co.) had been under a misapprehension. Whilst the figure of £360 had been put forward as a 'reasonable estimate', the GCR had no intention of undertaking the work; only giving guidance about the cost. The Railway Signalling Co. was approached again, as it had tendered £475 for the work. The Engineer managed to get the price down to £450. In October, Walters Electrical Co. won the contract to install needle block instruments and telephones.

Another Bill

Once again the matter of the projected branches came up when, in October, the company's solicitors reported that it would be necessary to apply to Parliament in the 1914 session for further capital powers to go ahead with the Kirkby Junction and western curve at Clipstone. It was deemed desirable to include powers to construct the Clipstone connection and the Rufford branch. A decision was made to convene a special meeting to settle the 'definite shape' of the Bill. Railway No. 1 in *this* Bill is the modification to the southerly junction at Kirkby (*see map page 34*). The projected cost was £4,934 but account had to be taken in this figure of the abandonment of the cost of Railway No. 1 in the 1910 Bill in so far as this affected the modification. (Section No. 1 of the original Bill was, by this time, already under construction.) Railway No. 2 was a branch to Clipstone Colliery. This branch would be 3 furlongs and 9 chains long and would sweep in a westerly direction from the main line. The projected cost for this was £4,091. Railway No. 3 was another branch to Clipstone Colliery. This branch, at a cost of £2,166, was 2 furlongs and 70 chains long and left the main line at Railway No. 2 but then turned in an easterly direction. Railway No. 4 was the Rufford Colliery branch which at a length of 2 miles, 1 furlong and 1 chain would cost £20,393. Last but certainly not least, a very important section, Railway No. 5, which was the western curve at Clipstone; the cost being £3,942. An additional amount of £1,000 was included for purchase of other lands. There was no serious opposition. The GCR now expressed an interest in the old vicarage at Mansfield, suggesting the company (GCR) could use part of it for much needed office accommodation until permanent offices could be made.

Meanwhile, the Engineer was becoming concerned about the slow progress of the work. In September, he complained to the contractors. The Board was even less satisfied and urged him to write a stronger letter. Another possible branch the company considered building was to a proposed colliery near Farnsfield but by November it was agreed the time was not right to seek such powers. Instead, Lord Savile would be approached in the hope that he might be favourably disposed in the future. Following a meeting at Dean's Yard, Westminster, on 11th December the solicitors went ahead with a Bill to provide

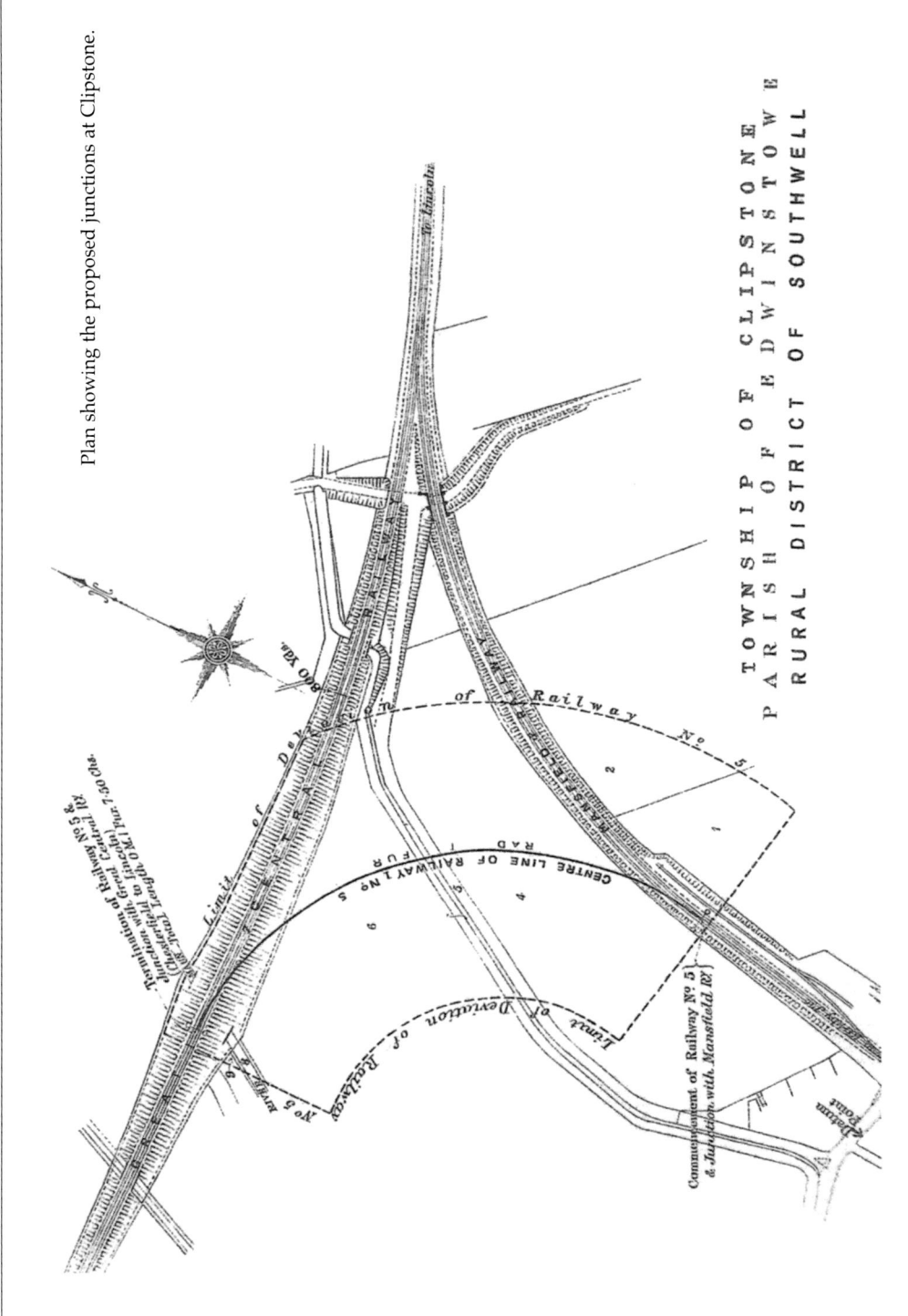

Plan showing the proposed junctions at Clipstone.

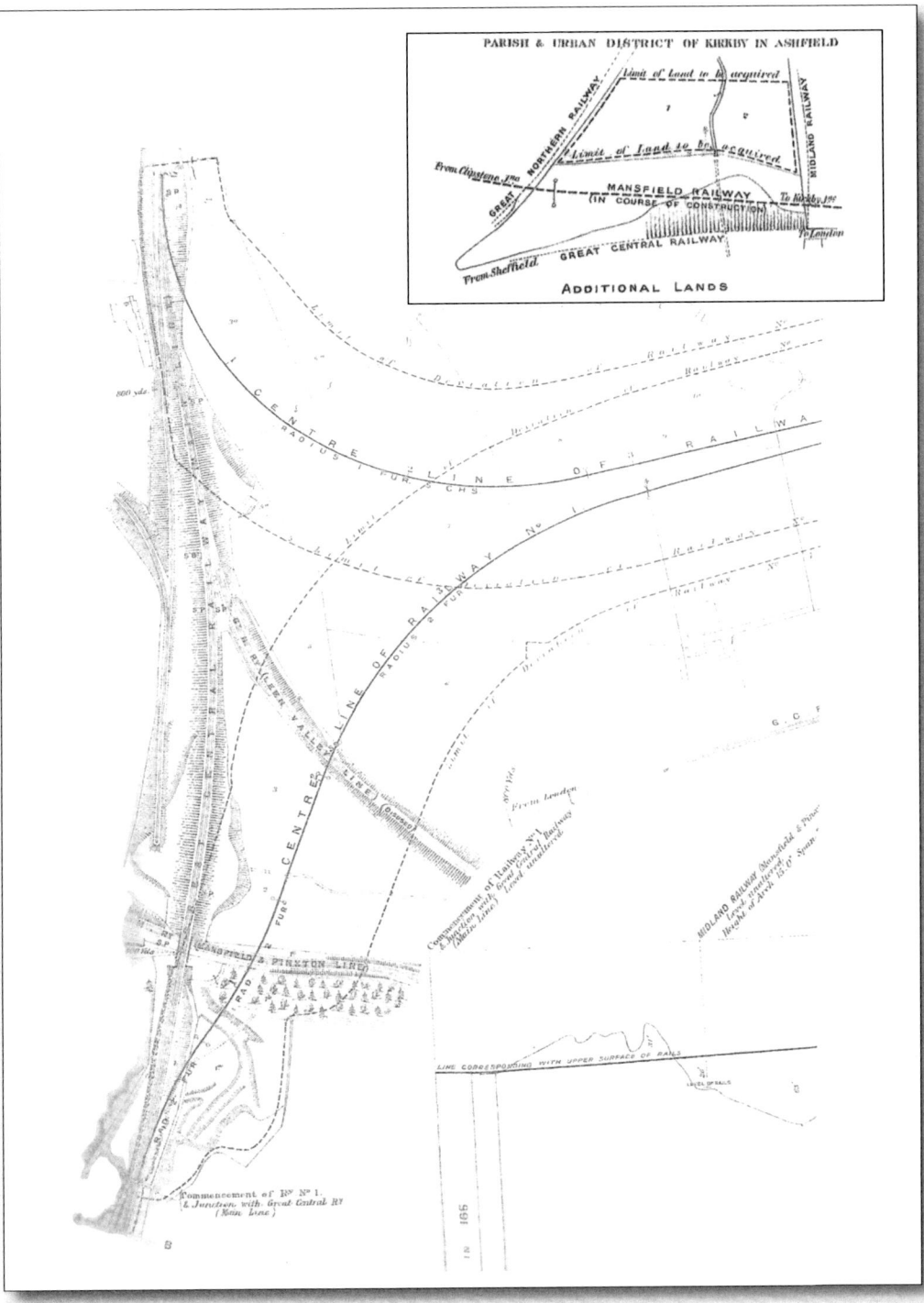

Proposed junctions at Kirkby. The scheme for the northern junction was abandoned.

[4 & 5 GEO. 5.] *Mansfield Railway Act,* 1914. **[Ch. xl.]**

CHAPTER xl.

An Act to confer further powers upon the Mansfield Railway Company with reference to the construction of works and the acquisition of lands and for other purposes. [8th July 1914.]

A.D. 1914.

WHEREAS by the Mansfield Railway Act 1910 (hereinafter referred to as "the Act of 1910") the Mansfield Railway Company (hereinafter called "the Company") were incorporated and authorised to make the railways and works in the county of Nottingham therein described and to raise two hundred and fifty thousand pounds partly by ordinary and partly by preference shares and to borrow on mortgage or raise by means of debenture stock eighty-three thousand three hundred and thirty-three pounds:

And whereas the Company have since the passing of the Act of 1910 created and issued the said capital of two hundred and fifty thousand pounds by the creation and issue of twelve thousand five hundred preference shares of ten pounds each and twelve thousand five hundred ordinary shares of ten pounds each and have created the sum of seventy-eight thousand pounds debenture stock and have constructed and opened for traffic a portion of their authorised railways:

And whereas it is expedient and would be of public and local advantage that the Company should be empowered to construct the extension railways described in this Act and to raise additional capital and borrow further money for the purpose in manner hereinafter mentioned:

And whereas it is expedient that the Company should have power as hereinafter provided to abandon a portion of Railway No. 1 authorised by the Act of 1910 rendered unnecessary by

[*Price* 1s. 9d.]   A   1

additional capital of £120,000, half in preference shares and half in ordinary shares. By the time this meeting was held, the Chairman had been able to see Lord Savile's representatives regarding the Rufford branch and his lordship had agreed to support the Bill and to sell his land for £75 per acre. A proposal to widen the road at Mansfield station to 36 ft, at a cost of £817, was accepted and it was resolved that because there would be a benefit to Mansfield Corporation the latter should be asked to meet additional costs. Sketch drawings of Kirkby station were approved and the making of detailed drawings authorized.

1914 – In spite of oppostion the Bill becomes an Act

In January it was possible to report that the Bill before Parliament had passed standing orders unopposed. On 9th February, agreements with the GCR regarding the Concentration Sidings, the western curve, Clipstone Colliery branch and the Kirkby Junction extension were all settled. The monies allocated for the Concentration Sidings were in two sums; the first of £18,128 and the second of £24,878, the latter only to be used to carry out the work when it was felt to be justified. Further negotiations went ahead involving the Rufford branch. The Bolsover Colliery Co. informed the Mansfield Railway Co. that it anticipated 250,000 extra tons would need to be moved out once coal was being mined. The other welcome news was that the time for petitioning against the Bill, currently going through, had expired and the only petition lodged was a joint one by the Butterley Co. and the Mining Association of Great Britain. The feeling was that these would not prove a serious threat and this turned out to be the case.

The Bill was read for the first time in the House of Lords on 10th February and it was then grouped with others to come before a select committee on Tuesday 28th April, 1914. On this occasion the Earl of Lytton was Chairman and, with a touch of legal irony, it was Mr Talbot (who had opposed the Mansfield Railway Bill on behalf of the Midland in 1910) who now represented the Mansfield Railway Co. The joint petitioners against the Bill attacked it vigorously. In spite of this it was resolved to increase the capital authorized to £150,000, with £75,000 to be preference shares. When the Bill came to the House of Commons there was a further objection, this time from the GNR, which opposed the plan to take land from that company at Kirkby-in Ashfield. The GNR argued that the move would seriously injure it and would affect arrangements with the GCR. A counter claim that the objection was vexatious lead to the GNR withdrawing the complaint. The Act is dated 8th July, 1914. The maintenance contract for Section 2 now came up for renewal and the GCR expressed a desire to take this from the contractors. This was agreed, although the GCR actually took over rather more than Section 2 and so paid the contractors compensation.

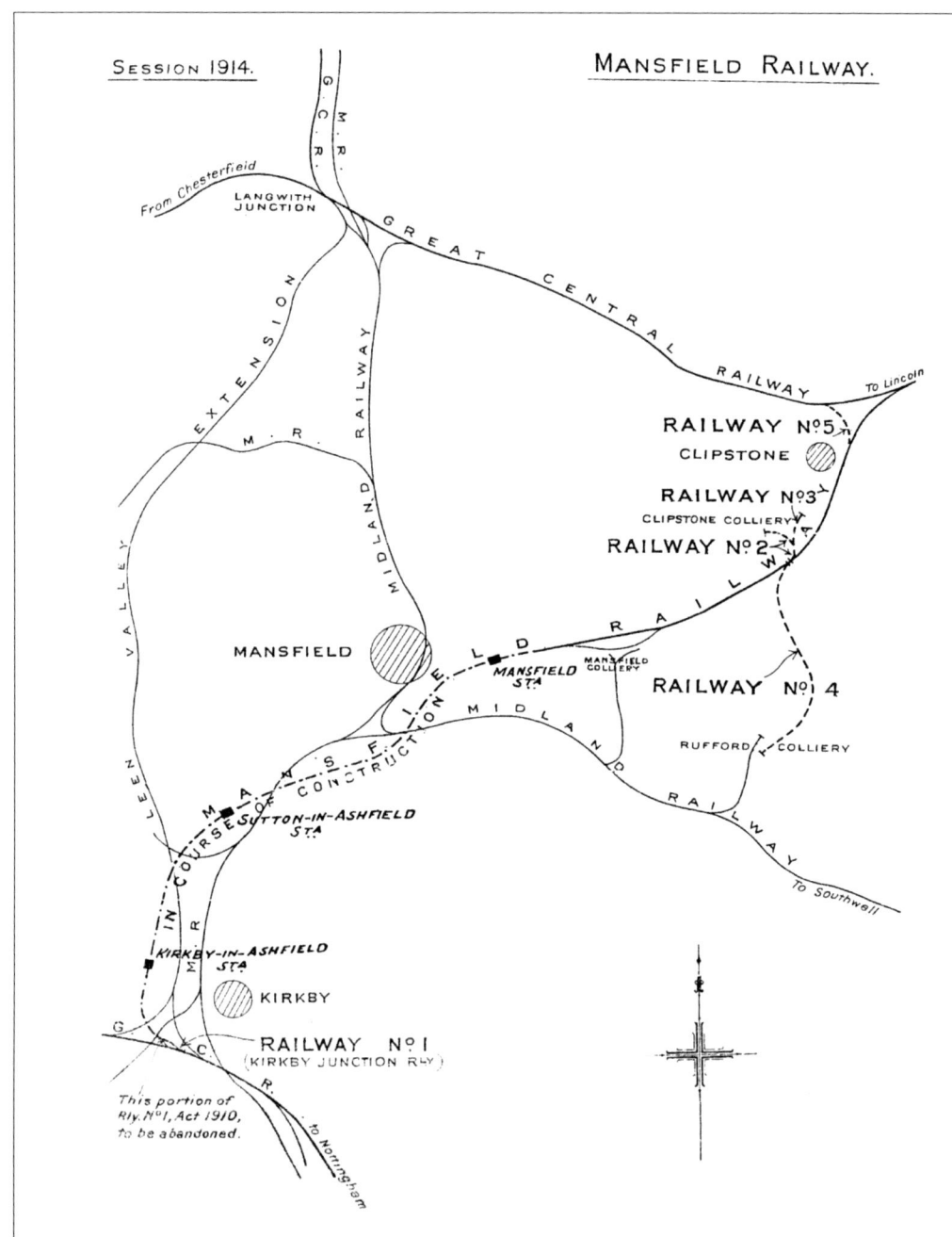

Mansfield session 1914 map

THE SCHEME GETS UNDERWAY, 1910-1917

Sam Fay has some reservations

With the gradual move towards the opening of the line in its entirety, there is evidence that latterly Sam Fay (strictly, by now, Sir Sam Fay – he was knighted in 1912, following the opening of the Immingham Docks in July of that year) had been having certain reservations about the way in which the line, once fully opened, would be controlled. It will be remembered that at the meeting of the select committee when giving evidence he had, it seems, to some extent, been pressed into agreeing that the line would be used to facilitate journeys between Mansfield and London. This having been agreed he had later become apprehensive about the fact that Elliott-Cooper had decided to use 'ordinary mechanical signalling' as opposed to track circuiting. In view of this, at the beginning of January, he wrote to the Board of Trade expressing his concerns.

> A question has arisen between this company [GCR] and the Mansfield Company as to the signalling that should be provided and I am given to understand that Mr Elliott-Cooper, the engineer, has been to the Board of Trade to consult one of the inspecting officers and has what he, Mr Elliott-Cooper, considers assent to ordinary mechanical signalling being provided.
> The Mansfield line will be an express line and undoubtedly carry heavy mineral and local passenger traffic and the GCR was desirous of track circuiting being provided throughout.

He goes on to point out that he realizes it may be difficult to enforce this change given the decision based on the consultation Elliott-Cooper has had with the Board of Trade but wishes to know whether this is what the Board would really want on a line of this type. He expresses concern that when it comes to the inspection there may be a decision to call for alterations to be made to the system and this would result, in effect, to money having been wasted.

The reply that Fay received was clearly not to his liking because in April he wrote again with feeling,

> I cannot say that I am satisfied with the position in which the GCR finds itself. If this line had been constructed by my company, the signalling would have been controlled by track circuiting throughout but in consequence of the Engineer submitting a plan or plans of some portion only of the line to the Board of Trade inspectors and obtaining approval of ordinary mechanical signalling the general arrangements will not be such as we should desire. I do think that a definite line should be taken by the Board of Trade on the subject of track circuiting especially when it is remembered that the General Managers were hauled up before the President of the Board of Trade on a recent occasion and were questioned as to what the companies were doing and proposing to do with regards to providing improved appliances, which appliances (more particularly track circuiting) are needed.

Fay continues with a caveat about the necessity to have this type of arrangement especially where there is slow moving mineral traffic with the occasional express and local passenger services.

He clearly sees this 'twelve miles of track' as part of a greater whole whereas Elliott-Cooper, it would seem, is simply looking at a 12 mile stretch in isolation,

'As I have said before, it is essentially a place where the greatest care should be taken in providing appliances to obviate the chances of signalmen making mistakes'. He concludes by stating that whilst he does not wish to put the Mansfield Company to unnecessary expense, he does want to see a modern and satisfactory system of signalling established on the Mansfield Railway before the GCR starts to work the line.

Fay then suggested to Elliott-Cooper that he should resubmit the plans for the Board of Trade to look again at the proposals.

2nd June, 1914 – The second section is opened – Mansfield to Mansfield Colliery

The section from Mansfield to Mansfield Colliery opened for traffic on 2nd June and this included the goods station at Mansfield (although, according to Haig-Brown's report, it was only partially opened at this stage) where two cranes and weighing machines had been installed. Thomas Turner of Langwith Lodge became a Director of the company in the same month. Further, the Act opened the way to raising new capital. Nine tenders were received for the building of the other stations and these ranged from £9,798 to £12,662. The lowest was submitted by John Greenwood of Mansfield and this was accepted. The GCR then expressed a desire to have additional sidings at Clipstone at a cost of £1,300 but it was felt this would only be possible if other sidings were deleted from the plan. As it happened, the specifications for the Rufford branch, Clipstone colliery sidings and the Concentration Sidings at Clipstone had been finalized and Baldry, Yerburgh and Hutchinson had already quoted for the work. However, the company felt it desirable to ask for further tenders. An approach was made to the company by Longden of Stanton Ironworks asking for the construction of a branch to a new Farnsfield Colliery at Kirklington and in reply the Board pointed out it was sympathetic to the scheme and would give it consideration.

By 12th August, Greenwood had encountered problems. It proved necessary to convene a special meeting of the Board as he wished his tender to be reviewed and he also sought an interview to discuss certain provisions. The outcome was that only the goods station and passenger station at Mansfield were to be undertaken at this point. In September, one of the outcomes of war was an increase in the cost of materials and the Board reluctantly recognized this and accepted it. Meantime, Baldry, Yerburgh and Hutchinson agreed to work with the price quoted in the previous June for the work. By November, another problem was becoming apparent; the shortage of manpower. The war had made demands in this respect and labour became more and more difficult to find.

THE SCHEME GETS UNDERWAY, 1910-1917 37

1915

In January 1915, the GCR made a request for 12 houses for the accommodation of staff at the Concentration Sidings and it was suggested these should be built privately and leased to the company. These were never built. The GCR also decided to seek Parliamentary powers to subscribe £25,000 towards the company's capital.

Also in January, it was agreed that tenders should be invited for the Rufford branch. On 15th April, the range of the seven tenders received was found to be considerable, the highest being £99,008. The figure of £32,172, submitted by Baldry, Yerburgh and Hutchinson was accepted.

In June, the Board of Trade informed the company that it did, in fact, require some modifications to the signalling and track circuiting throughout and problems arose in October when the Butterley company was held responsible for causing subsidence and damage to the line. On 13th June the Clipstone Colliery branch came into use. In that month, also, traffic advisor Haig Brown submitted a report to the Directors of the Mansfield Railway dealing mainly with returns and financial projections. Amongst other things, he was able to inform them that in the last 18 months, the traffic conveyed over the section opened to Clipstone Junction had considerably exceeded the estimate. In general the financial outlook was very encouraging. Haig Brown was clearly very optimistic.

Government control

On the outbreak of war (later referred to as World War I) the control of the railway system passed into Government control under 'The Powers of the Regulation of the Forces Act 1871'. The date the power was invoked was 4th August and it had been agreed that dividends set should be based on previous (1913) performance. The Mansfield Railway found itself with something of a dilemma. First, because it was not informed that the company had been taken over but only later discovered that it had been included in the regulation as applied to the GCR, the company working the line; second, because only part of the line was open it was deemed unfair to base any dividend on performance in these circumstances. Sanders, the company's Secretary, wrote to the Secretary for State for War pointing out what was felt to be an anomaly. He expressed the view that the Directors should receive the figures for the half year ending 1913-14 with an additional £1,400; in total £4,000 for the period covering the Government control. For the period up to June 1915 a figure of £1,000 per month should be paid. When the line was fully open this figure should be increased to £1,750 with a further allowance once passenger services were started. He was keen to point out that £400,000 had already been expended on the line and a further £100,000 would be spent on its completion and also that the link to be established would enable Admiralty coal to be transported from South Wales and the South to Grimsby and East Coast ports so giving the line strategic 'Military and Admiralty' importance. There was also the matter of the Army Camp being planned for Clipstone.

The case Sanders made was seen as a strong one; the Railway Executive Committee agreed to pay up.

A postcard view of the army camp that was built during World War I at Clipstone. The camp was served by the railway. *Author's Collection*

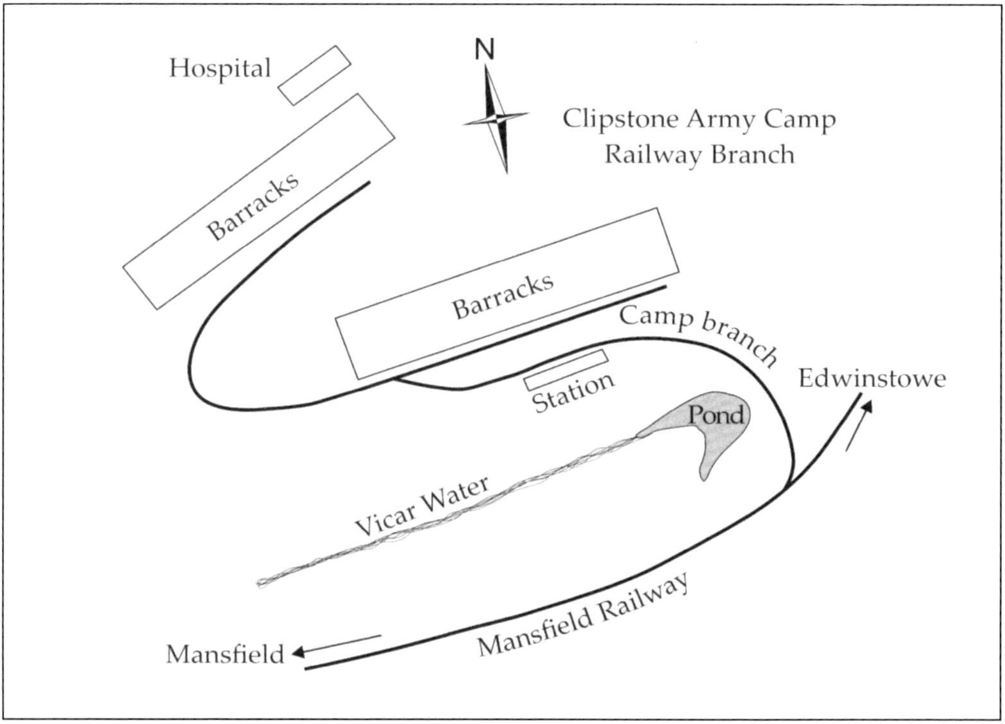

The army camp at Clipstone

The start of the war had a considerable impact on the Mansfield Railway, coming, as it did, when the railway was very much in the construction stage. Reference has been made to the problems experienced because there was a shortage of able-bodied men as more and more were called up for active service and the slowing down of the progress which resulted. Another aspect was the decision to create a large military camp at Clipstone, where army personnel could be assembled and, to some extent, trained before being sent off to fight in the trenches in what was to prove a bitter and bloody engagement. This camp was situated in the vicinity of the newly emerging Clipstone Colliery and it was inevitable that, although construction was the responsibility of the military authorities, the Mansfield Railway would become a strategic element in providing communications for the installation. By the early part of 1915 over 700 huts had been erected and it was anticipated these would accommodate 12 battalions of infantry (about 12,000 men) and more were expected. Initially troops coming to the camp would alight at Mansfield and then march to the camp. Again, Eric Brailsford witnessed this happening. 'I remember very vividly seeing the soldiers being brought into Mansfield station G.C. They didn't come down through the station they just jumped down the embankments'.

Although the rail link was completed by mid-June 1915, a passenger service, was not introduced until 1st October, 1917 following the introduction of general passenger traffic in April of that year. The GCR did not assume full responsibility for the branch until 17th December, 1917. A Memorandum was issued by the War Office to the GCR relating to this date. In this document there is a number of clauses giving the various conditions which would be applied to the operation. These clauses dealt with a variety of aspects including the expenses which would be incurred.

> All the expenses of the Company [The GCR] in connection with the Camp Railway [the title given by the War Office] and all receipts, if any, derived by them therefrom shall be deemed to be part of the expenses and receipts of the Company for ascertaining the compensation due to the Company under the 'Regulation of the Forces Act 1871'. Expenditure incurred on maintenance shall be charged to the Railway Company's working expenses in account with the Government under the separate head of 'Work done for the Government'.

Other clauses refer to possible construction of additional sidings, platforms and buildings, permanent way materials and stores, essentially requiring full inventories to be kept. The War Department locomotives and rolling stock would be at the disposal of the GCR but when handed back, once the War Office ceased to use the facility, should be returned 'in equally good condition, fair wear and tear excepted'. The document is ratified by Brigadier-General Ben Atkinson CB CMG for the War Office and Sam Fay for the GCR.

The camp line was constructed from the main line, just to the east of Vicar Pond and formed an 's' shape to the north with a short branch from this in the centre section and extending eastwards. The station for the camp was on a short spur which extended westwards just to the north of Vicar Pond. There was no return loop. The facilities were not really adequate enough to accommodate large troop movements and it seems the plan was for troops to alight at Mansfield (as previously mentioned, eye-witnesses report seeing troops leaving the station) or Edwinstowe and march the rest of the journey. The platform was very basic, being made up of little more than earth piled to the appropriate height and retained by using railway sleepers. A ticket office was provided and the 'station' was soon in great use, so much so that additional trains to Mansfield were provided. There is a photograph in existence showing a train hauled by a GCR Robinson Atlantic (4-4-2) waiting at the camp. The branch was worked using the staff system operated from the signal box at the junction on the main line. When the war finished, the camp was used as a dispersal centre and so the railway remained for a time. Eventually camp and railway were dismantled and the only tangible evidence remaining consisted of the trenches where training had been carried out and these, it is said, were still visible many years later. There is still a 'Station Road' in Clipstone. The origin of this seems a little obscure. It might be assumed it relates to the station at the army camp as there was no other station built in the colliery village. However, in view of its location, there have been suggestions that it was hoped Clipstone would be worthy of a station and there was a petition to this end. Naming 'Station Road' was possibly a premature move; the result of some wishful thinking on somebody's part?

A contemporary cartoon captioned, 'Come and renew your childhood at sunny, bracing Clipstone'.

THE SCHEME GETS UNDERWAY, 1910-1917

1916 – The line opens throughout for goods traffic

In January 1916 the contractors were taken to task because the date for the completion of Section 2, 1st December, 1915, had long passed. The company threatened to impose a fine of £100 per week for the delay but the contractor pleaded 'war conditions' as the reason and it was agreed that the Chairman should meet the contractor.

With the opening impending it was considered necessary to have a 'Further Agreement' with the Mansfield company, the GCR and the Bolsover company. The amendment related to the fact that the Mansfield company had abandoned Railway No. 1 in the original Act and referred thereafter to the 'Kirkby Junction Railway.' It was also in connection with the Bolsover company having acquired an additional area of coal near Clipstone and the plan to sink a further pit in the vicinity. On 23rd March an agreement was drawn up which enabled the Bolsover company to have a possible 250,000 tons of coal per annum carried out by the Mansfield - GCR railway (it later transpired this was in respect of Rufford Colliery) irrespective of the 500,000 tons per annum stipulated in the 1910 agreement (this was in respect of Mansfield and Clipstone collieries). A further amendment in an Agreement signed the following day was, in part, a very fine tuning exercise, the Bolsover company having insisted that the clause in Section 2 of the Agreement of 31st October, 1910 should be modified to read 'sent by way of the Kirkby Junction Railway authorized by the Mansfield Railway Act 1914'. There was also a clause verifying the allowances in rates as previously agreed.

The line was ready by July and Sam Fay made an inspection of the whole railway from Kirkby- in-Ashfield to Clipstone and expressed a willingness to take over the working for goods and mineral trains from 4th September. Initially this would be from Mansfield Goods (depot) and Kirkby South Junction. On this day Mr J. Rostern, the chief goods manager at Marylebone, wrote a letter to the Mansfield Railway Co. This was in reply to one he had received on 28th August. It referred to the fact that this letter had made reference to traffic with Mansfield Line stations only. However, information was requested about particulars of trains that it was proposed would be diverted over the line and the instructions relating to these. These trains were clearly going to form an important element of the traffic conveyed on the line. Once the line opened, on 4th September, a considerable volume of traffic was reported. A formal opening of the line had been considered but it was agreed at this stage that the considerable expense involved could not be justified and would be inappropriate as a war was still being fought. The introduction of passenger traffic was now high on the agenda but the GCR was adamant that the lifts, still needed at Mansfield station, should be installed first. These lifts had to be brought over from America where they had been made because pressure of Government work for the war effort made it impossible for them to be made in England. It was anticipated that the equipment would be in place and operational by 1st January, 1917.

In March Haig Brown was clearly uneasy and in a letter to Sanders he pointed out that his revision of the estimates of income from the line did not appear to have been passed on to Sam Fay.

Circular No. 5390.

GREAT CENTRAL RAILWAY.

OPENING OF THE MANSFIELD RAILWAY BETWEEN MANSFIELD GOODS STATION AND KIRKBY SOUTH JUNCTION.

MONDAY, SEPTEMBER 4th, 1916.

Referring to Circular No. 5373 dated June 12th, 1913, and Special Traffic Arrangements and Engineering Works Notice (N. & E.D., No. 43) for Week ending June 6th, 1914.

On Monday, September 4th, 1916, the remaining portion of the Mansfield Railway between Mansfield Goods Station and Kirkby South Junction will be opened for through Goods and Coal traffic. The intermediate Stations, viz.:—Sutton-in-Ashfield and Kirkby-in-Ashfield will not be opened at present.

This portion of the Line which consists of two lines of rails, is approximately five miles in length. The line from Mansfield Goods Station to Kirkby South Junction will be designated the Up Line, and that from Kirkby South Junction to Mansfield Station the Down Line. The Line will be worked in accordance with the Block Telegraph Regulations for working on double lines of railway and the section will be between Mansfield Goods Station and Kirkby South Junction.

The speed of trains must not exceed 12 miles per hour.

A diagram of the Line shewing the gradients is annexed hereto.

The loads for Goods and Mineral engines between **Mansfield Goods Station and Kirkby South Junction** will be as under:—

UP OR DOWN.

No. 1 Class.			No. 2 Class.			No. 3 Class.			No. 4 Class.			No. 5 Class.		
G.	M.	E.	G.	M.	E.	G.	M.	E.	G.	M.	E.	G.	M.	E.
61	46	90	48	35	65	45	32	60	43	31	55	35	25	40

The following trains will be diverted and run via Mansfield:—

The 5.30 p.m Special Express Fish Train Grimsby Docks to London (S.) will be retimed as under.

	Mons. & Thurs.	Tues. & Weds. & Fris.
	p.m.	
Grimsby Docks ....dep.	5 30	
Barnetby ....pass	6 0	
Pelham Street ....pass	6 40	
Pyewipe Junction ....pass	6 47	
Clipstone Junction ....pass	7 23	
Mansfield ....pass	7 55	
Kirkby South Junction ....pass	8 0	
Annesley ....pass	8 5	
Bagthorpe Junction ....pass	8 10	
Nottingham (Vic.) ....arr.	—	8 21
" " ....pass	8 21	—
" " ....dep.	—	8 31
" " Goods ....arr.	8 25	—
" " ....dep.	8 42	—
Leicester Pass....................arr.	—	9 15
" " ....pass	9 18	—
" " ....dep.	—	9 40
Woodford..........................arr.	10 16	10 45
" " ....dep.	10 26	11 0
Brackley	T ‡	T ‡
Quainton Road ....pass	11 5	11 40

and forward as shewn in working time table dated July 14th.

‡ 2 minutes allowed.

The 6.15 p.m Special Express Fish Train Grimsby Docks to London will run when required on Mondays and Thursdays in addition to Saturdays, and will be retimed as under :—

		p.m.			p.m.
Grimsby Docks	dep.	6 5	Woodford	arr.	11 30
Barnetby	pass	6 57			midn't.
	(slow road)		,,	dep.	12 0
Pelham Street	pass	7 22			a.m.
Pyewipe Junction	pass	7 28	Quainton Road	pass	12 37
Clipstone Junction	pass	8 2	Aylesbury	pass	12 48
Mansfield	pass	8 14	Chalfont Road	pass	1 14
Kirkby South Junction	pass	8 30	Rickmansworth	pass	1 24
Annesley	pass	8 42	Harrow	pass	1 38
Bagthorpe Junction	pass	8 55	Neasden Junction	pass	1 46
Nottingham (Vic.)	arr.	9 0	Marylebone	arr.	1 57
,, ,,	dep.	9 10			
Leicester (Passr.)	arr.	9 55			
,,	dep.	10 25			

The 6.45 p.m. Special Express Fish Train from Grimsby Docks to London (Mondays and Thursdays only) will not run.

The 8.20 p.m. Express Goods Grimsby Docks to Bulwell will be retimed between Tuxford and Annesley as shown below :—

	arr.	pass	dep.
Tuxford West	—	11 5 p.m.	—
Ollerton		T	
Clipstone Junction	—	11 28	—
Mansfield Goods	11 43	—	11 58
Kirkby South Junction	—	12 23	—
Annesley	12 28 a.m.	—	

The following trains will be retimed between Annesley and Tuxford West as shown below :—

(1) 12.45 a.m. Fish empties Neasden to Grimsby Docks (M.O.)
(2) 7.35 p.m. Fish empties Marylebone to Grimsby Docks.
(3) 11.35 p.m. Express Goods Marylebone to Grimsby (Wednesdays only).

	1 MO	2 Tues. to Sun. inclusive	3 Thurs. only.
	a.m.	a.m.	a.m.
Annesley pass	...	1 37	...
,, dep.	5 30	...	8 25
Kirkby South Jc. pass	5 36	1 42	8 31
Mansfield Goods arr.	—	—	8 57
,, ,, dep.	X	X	9 10
Clipstone Junc. pass	6 26	2 33	9 50
Ollerton	W	W	W. & T.
Tuxford	X	...	...
Tuxford West arr.	...	2 48	...
,, ,, pass	6 55	...	10 0
,, ,, dep.	...	3 0	...

The trains will run forward as shewn in the working time table dated July 14th.

The 3.45 p.m. coal train between Mansfield Colliery and Banbury (Wednesdays only) will be retimed to Annesley as shewn below :—

		p.m.
Mansfield Colliery	dep.	3 55
,, Goods	pass	4 5
Kirkby South Junction	pass	4 31
Annesley	arr.	4 36

A new Coal train will run between Annesley Sidings and Mansfield Colliery as under :—

WEEKDAYS.

	arr. p.m.	dep. p.m.		arr. p.m.	dep. p.m.
Annesley Sidings...............	—	4 10	Mansfield Colliery	—	6 10
Kirkby South Junction	4 16		Mansfield Goods	6 20	6 35
Mansfield Goods	4 42	5 10	Kirkby South Junction	7 1	
Mansfield Colliery	5 20	—	Annesley Sidings...............	7 7	—

The following Signal alterations will be brought into use :—

MANSFIELD STATION.

A signal box, which will be known as "Mansfield Station," has been erected by the side of the Up Shunting Neck at 5 miles 20 chains.

The following points and signals will be worked from the signal box.

A connection in the Down Main Line 118 yards west of the signal box leading to Down Siding with trap points in same at fouling with Down Main Line.

A through connection between the Up Sidings 140 yards west of the signal box, and Down Main Line 48 yards West of the signal box, with slip connection in same forming Main Line West Crossover road, and double slip connection giving access to Up Shunting Neck.

A through connection between Down Main 47 yards West of the signal box and Wharf Siding and run-round line with slip connection in same opposite the signal box giving access with Up Main, and a double slip connection 88 yards East of the signal box giving access to bay line, or shunting neck.

Trap points in shunting neck opposite the signal box.

Trap points in run-round line and Wharf Siding at the fouling with bay line.

A connection in bay line 217 yards East of the signal box leading to run-round line with trap points in the same at fouling with bay line.

DOWN SIGNALS.

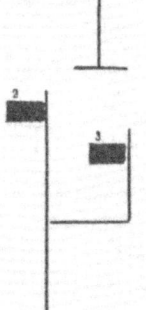

Erected by the side of Down Main Line 1,584 yards West of the signal box.

1. Down Main Distant.

Erected by the side of Down Main Line 167 yards West of the signal box.

2. Down Main Home.
3. Down Main to Bay Line.

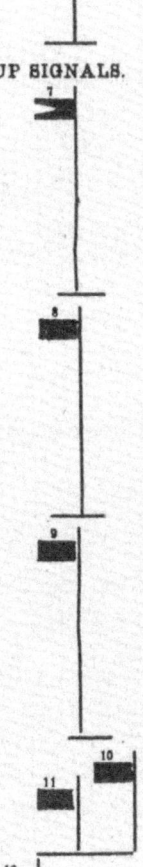

Erected by the side of Down Main Line 844 yards East of the signal box.

4. Down Main Inner Home.

Erected by the side of Down Siding opposite Down main Home Signal.

5. Down Siding to Down Main.
6. Down Siding to Bay or carriage dock.

UP SIGNALS.

Erected between Up Siding and Up Main 1847 yards East of the signal box.

7. Up Main Distant.

Erected by the side of Up Main Line 407 yards East of the signal box.

8. Up Main Home.

Erected by the side of Down Main Line 58 yards East of the signal box.

9. Up Main Inner Home.

Erected by the side of trap points in Wharf Siding and run-round line 70 yards East of the signal box.

10. Bay Line to Up Main.
11. Bay Line to Shunting neck.
12. Run-round Line or Wharf Siding to Shunting neck.
13. Run-round Line or Wharf Siding to Up Main.

Erected between shunting neck and Up Main Line 454 yards West of the signal box.

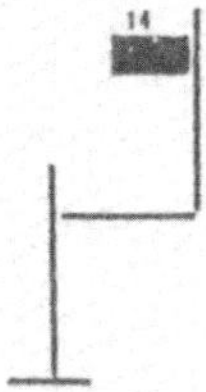

14. Up Main Starter.

Erected between Up Main and Up Sidings 167 yards West of the signal box.

15. Up Sidings, Group 1 to Down Main.

16. Up Sidings, Group 1 to Shunting neck.

Erected between Up Sidings Groups 1 and 2 opposite above signal.

17. Up Sidings, Group 2 to Down Main.

18. Up Sidings, Group 2 to shunting neck.

Erected by the side of shunting neck 87 yards West of the signal box.

19. Shunting neck to Up Sidings, Groups 1 or 2.

Disc signal fixed by the side of Down Main 113 yards West of the signal box will apply from Down Main to Down Siding.

Disc signal fixed between Up and Down Main Lines at West end of Main Line Crossover road will apply from Up Main to Down Main.

Disc signal fixed by the side of Down Main at the East end of Main Line crossover road will apply from Down Main to Up Sidings, Group 1 and 2, Up Main, or Down Siding.

Disc signal fixed between Up Main and shunting neck 20 yards West of the signal box will apply from Up Main to bay line, run-round line, or wharf siding.

Disc signal fixed by the side of shunting neck trap points opposite the signal box will apply from shunting neck to bay line, run-round line, or wharf siding.

Disc signal fixed by the side of run-round line trap points 178 yards East of the signal box will apply from run-round line to bay line.

Disc signal fixed by the side of bay line 217 yards East of the signal box will apply from bay line to run-round line.

WEST END GROUND FRAME.

A ground frame erected by the side of shunting neck, slightly west of the 5-mile post, will control the outlet from shunting neck to Up Main Line, also a disc signal erected by the outlet points which will apply from shunting neck to Up Main Line.

EAST END GROUND FRAME.

A ground frame erected by the side of the Up Main Line, 348 yards east of the signal box, will control a Main Line crossover road laid in immediately east of the ground frame.

Both the above ground frames will be bolted from the signal box.

The signal box will be open from 5.30 a.m. until the passing of the 7.35 p.m. Fish Empties train from London to Grimsby.

KIRKBY SOUTH JUNCTION.

Facing points have been laid in the Down Main line, and trailing points in the Up Main line immediately South of the signal box, giving connection with the Mansfield Railway.

Temporary trap points have been laid in the Up and Down Mansfield lines at the fouling with Up Main line.

A clearance bar has been provided in the Down Mansfield line immediately East of the temporary trap points.

DOWN SIGNALS.

The Down Main Distant to the G.N. Branch fixed on Annesley North Junction Down Starter will be taken away.

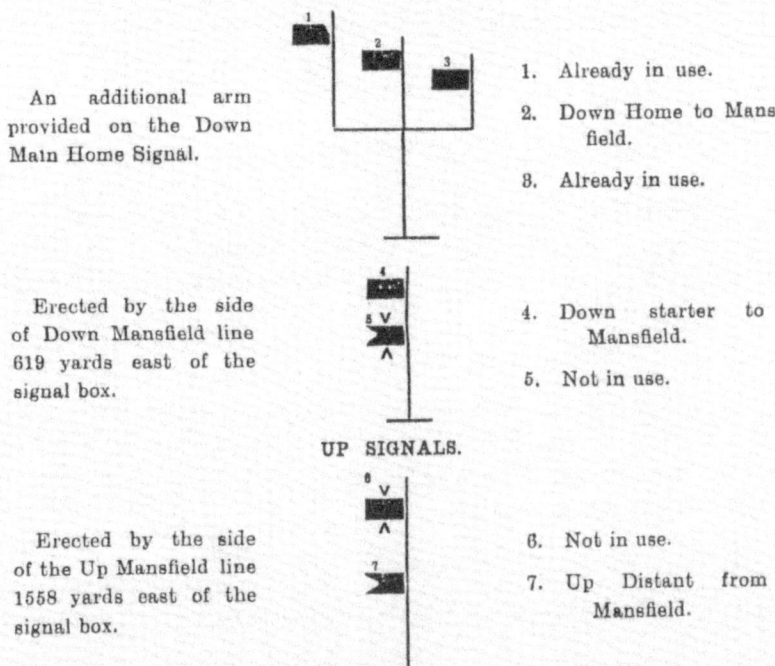

An additional arm provided on the Down Main Home Signal.

1. Already in use.
2. Down Home to Mansfield.
3. Already in use.

Erected by the side of Down Mansfield line 619 yards east of the signal box.

4. Down starter to Mansfield.
5. Not in use.

UP SIGNALS.

Erected by the side of the Up Mansfield line 1558 yards east of the signal box.

6. Not in use.
7. Up Distant from Mansfield.

Erected by the side of Down Mansfield line 550 yards east of the signal box.

8. Up outer home from Mansfield.

Erected by the side of Up Mansfield line opposite the Up Main Home Signal.

9. Up inner home from Mansfield.

The higher and lower disc signals fixed between the Up and Down Main Lines at the South end of the Main Line crossover Road will be superseded by three disc signals fixed by the side of the Up Main Line. The left hand disc will apply from Up Main to Down Main, the centre disc Up Main to Down Mansfield Line, and the right hand disc Up Main to Down G.N. Line.

Referring to Special Traffic Arrangements and Engineering Works Notice (N. & E. D.) No. 48 for week ending June 6th, 1914. On and from Monday next, the instructions respecting the working of trains between Mansfield Colliery Sidings Box and Mansfield Goods Yard will be withdrawn, and the trains will be worked over the Up and Down Lines in accordance with the Block Telegraph Regulations for working on double lines of railway.

Run-back points have been laid in the Down line immediately north of Kirkby South Junction Starting Signal.

Run-back points have been laid in the Up line 660 yards north of the Sutton-in-Ashfield Signal Box up outer Home Signal.

Run-back points have been laid in the Up line, 660 yards north of the Mansfield Colliery Signal Box up Outer Home Signal.

Run-back points have been laid in the Up line 660 yards north of the Concentration Sidings Signal Box up Home Signal.

Engine Whistles to be given by Drivers.

Engine Drivers of trains for the Mansfield Line at Kirkby South Junction must give one long and two short whistles when approaching Annesley South Junction signal box.

Engine Drivers when approaching Mansfield Station Box must give five short whistles when requiring to pass on to the Goods Line at Annesley North Junction and one long and two short whistles when requiring to pass on to the Goods Loop Line at Annesley North Junction.

The line (exclusive of Kirkby South Junction) will be included in the Eastern District under the control of Mr. F. PATMAN, Grimsby Docks.

THE SCHEME GETS UNDERWAY, 1910-1917

Further discussion involving the Bilsthorpe branch ensued in November. The Stanton company responsible for the colliery had not finalized its plans and so a decision was made not to press ahead with the branch, although a proposal to approach the Stanton company with a plan to construct a light railway the following May was considered.

From the outset there had been a proposal to operate 'express' fish trains from Grimsby and Hull along the Mansfield Railway.

With the line now opened for goods traffic these were rerouted. By way of an example, the following timetable, issued in 1916, gives the details of the operation for one of these trains.

When required on Mondays and Thursdays in addition to Saturdays

		pm
Grimsby	dep.	6.05
Barnetby	pass	6.37 (slow road)
Pelham Street	pass	7.22
Pyewipe Junction	pass	7.28
Clipstone Junction	pass	8.02
Mansfield	pass	8.14
Kirkby South Junction	pass	8.39
Annesley	pass	8.42
Bagthorpe Junction	pass	8.55
Nottingham Victoria	arr.	9.00
	dep.	9.10
Leicester (passenger)	arr.	9.55
	dep.	10.25
Woodford	arr.	11.30
		Midnight
	dep.	12.00
		am
Quainton Road	pass	12.37
Aylesbury	pass	12.48
Chalfont Road	pass	1.14
Rickmansworth	pass	1.24
Harrow	pass	1.38
Neasden Junction	pass	1.48
Marylebone	arr.	1.57

This service was later extended to meet wider demands (referred to later) with vans being dropped at other strategic points.

At this time it was also announced that a signal box, which would be known as Mansfield Station had been erected by the side of the 'Up shunting neck'.

The following instruction was given to drivers:

> Engine drivers of trains for the Mansfield Line at Kirkby South Junction must give one long and two short whistles when approaching Annesley South Junction signal box.
> Engine drivers when approaching Mansfield Station Box must give five short whistles when requiring to pass on to the Goods Line at Annesley North Junction and one long and two short whistles when requiring to pass onto the Goods Loop Line at Annesley North Junction.

THE MANSFIELD RAILWAY

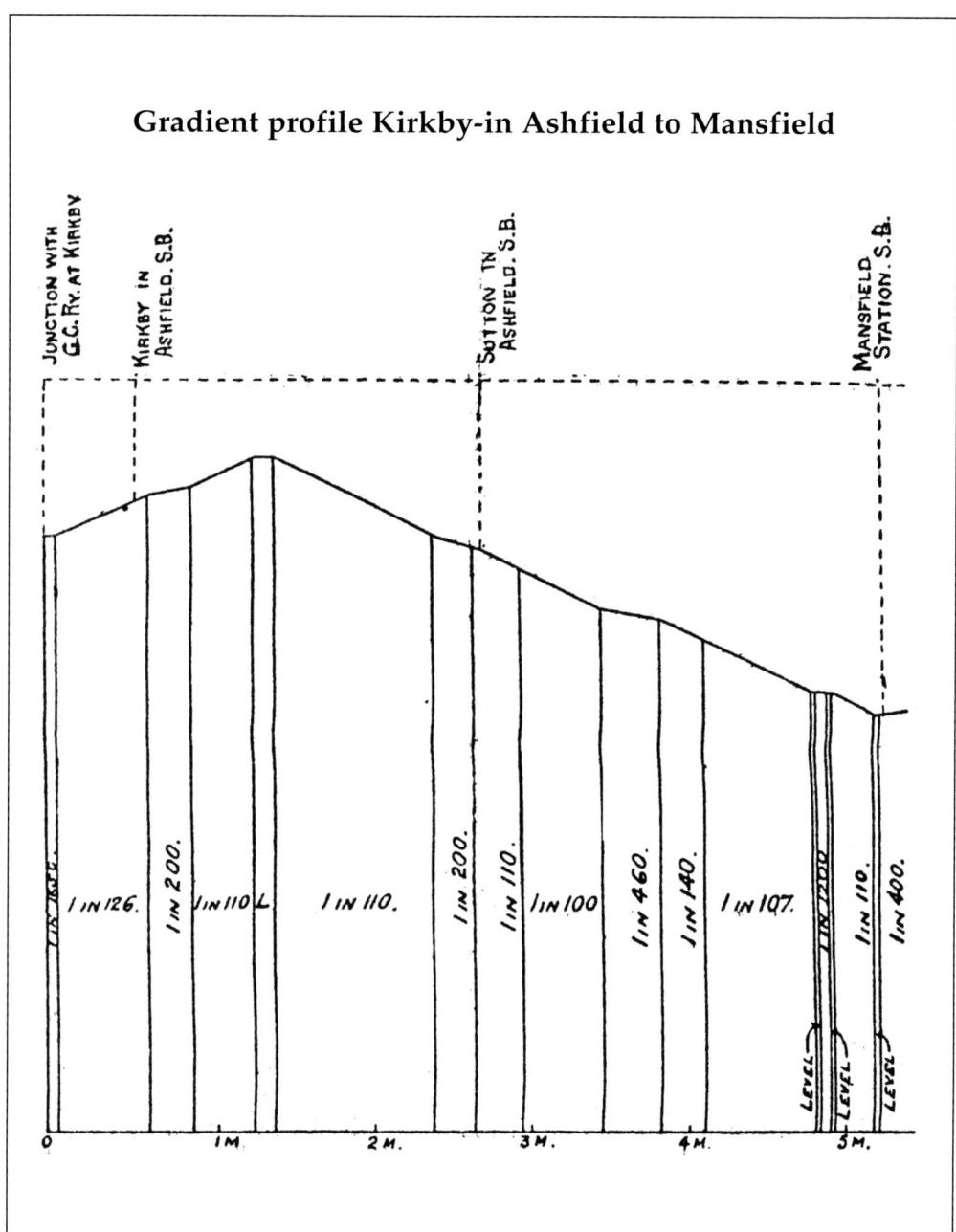

Accidents

By this stage, accidents on the line had been few. In September 1916 a report under the heading 'An Extraordinary Mischance' described how a man was killed 'whilst engaged on what was one of the safest jobs in the construction of a railway line to the Rufford Colliery'. Robert Preston, 63 years of age, was killed not by an engine but by a horse. Mr Preston was removing sleepers from the line near Rufford Junction. These sleepers had formed a temporary road and were being removed to make way for new ones. The sleepers were secured by a chain which was fastened to a horse. Five sleepers were being removed at a time. The horse stumbled and fell on Robert Preston and then rolled over him, killing him. It was said the horse 'was quiet and used to go to work and had never given any trouble'. A verdict of accidental death was returned by the jury. The following year, in November 1917, a platelayer, Jonathan Longden, aged 63, was killed by a light engine which knocked him down as it travelled tender first towards Clipstone. The driver, John Kidder, described the weather at the time of the accident (about 7.50 am) as 'rather hazy'. However, a luggage train had passed and the smoke and steam had obscured his view. The smoke had been particularly thick and when it cleared, the driver spotted a man just in front of the train. He had no time to sound the whistle but quickly applied the brakes. The driver was not sure whether the man had jumped clear but the fireman informed him that the man had been knocked down. Jonathan Longden's death was recorded as 'the first fatality to have occurred on the main line' so it would seem that Robert Preston was reckoned to be working on the branch.

1917 – A successful inspection

The line was ready for inspection by the beginning of 1917 and on 3rd and 4th January Colonel Pringle, of the Board of Trade, carried out an inspection. Subject to a few alterations, he passed the line as being fit for passenger traffic. There was, however, a proviso that a limit of 25 mph should be imposed until the banks had consolidated. The Engineer felt that the various modifications needed could be carried out to enable the line to open on 12th February. Meanwhile Sam Fay still had his eyes on the old vicarage at Mansfield station and in December of the previous year had asked that it be converted for use as a residence for the station agent because the original idea that it might have to be demolished and the site used for extending the sidings was no longer being considered. The building was made habitable at a cost of £265. The Engineer's prediction that the line would open on 12th February did not prove to be accurate but all was ready for the opening to be held on 2nd April. Although the Board had decided to avoid ostentatious ceremony, the Directors felt they could not let the occasion pass without yet more junketing.

Mansfield station frontage to Great Central Road on the upside. From a drawing by Jasper C. Meaden dated March 1914. *Railway News*

Sutton-in-Ashfield station buildings. The same type of buildings were adopted at Kirkby-in-Ashfield. From a drawing by Jasper C. Meaden dated March 1914. *Railway News*

Chapter Three

Another opening ceremony, 1917-1923

2nd April, 1917 – The railway opens to passenger trains

There can be few railways which had more than one opening ceremony, complete with feasting and long speeches. The Mansfield Railway is numbered amongst them; the Kendal & Windermere Railway is another which can claim a similar achievement.

A report in a local newspaper, the *Mansfield Advertiser*, tells us about the events of 2nd April and begins as follows:

> The opening of the new Mansfield Railway took place on Monday last in a very quiet and unostentatious manner. An event of so much importance to the town of Mansfield and surrounding district would no doubt in normal times have been marked by great rejoicing but it was deemed to be more in keeping with war-time to make Monday's proceedings a private and informal function.

The first train left Nottingham at 7.30 am and arrived at Mansfield at 8.15 am. It had passed through a snowstorm. The train then travelled over the rest of the line to the junction with the GCR just beyond Clipstone and so on to Edwinstowe and Ollerton. This train did not carry the members of the Board. They travelled on a special train which left Nottingham just before noon. Those travelling included Directors J.P. Houfton, T. Craven, W.J. Chadburn and F. Pilling, the Engineer, R. Elliott-Cooper, the resident engineer C.B. Swan, the Secretary, H.A. Sanders together with a number of officials from the GCR, among them J.G.Gibson, the superintendent of the line. En route the group made careful observations of the Concentration Sidings at Clipstone which were still under construction. The journey was reported as being a smooth one, although a speed restriction of 25 mph had been imposed until the line settled. In spite of the war, the event could not be allowed to pass without a lunch and the opportunity for some speeches. The venue for these was the Hop Pole Hotel in Ollerton. Houfton, as Chairman, presided and after the meal he first called on the assembled company to honour the toast to the King. Then followed the speeches. Oratory skills were exercised to the full. It was J.G. Gibson, of the GCR, who began by proposing a toast 'The success of the Mansfield Railway'. He pointed out how favourably impressed everybody had been by what they had seen and how the line was 'well and truly laid'. The shareholders were to be congratulated on supporting the far-seeing enterprise of the Directors. He went on to repeat these points as if to give them emphasis. He had high praise for the Secretary and the 'excellent' Engineer 'who had his heart and soul in the business'. His only misgiving, it seems, was that he felt Elliott-Cooper might have been a little more far seeing and laid four lines rather than two because he [Gibson] felt sure one day these would be required. However, in a spirit of magnanimity he conceded that everyone makes mistakes! The contractors having been praised and the hope expressed that although the present limit was

25 mph, expresses would soon be using the line, the toast was drunk 'with cordiality'.

Houfton replied. Once again, he seemed in a rather less magnanimous mood, at least as far as the GCR was concerned. What seems to have upset him a little was Gibson's lack of reference to the benefits the Mansfield Railway would bring to Gibson's company (the GCR) and Houfton was quick to redress this by saying that what Gibson had *not* said was of greater weight than what he had! 'He has never once referred to the benefit that the Mansfield Railway Company would be to the Great Central'. Not satisfied with having said this, he went further. He made it clear that in his experience railway companies were ready to take everything given them without thanks and perhaps Mr Gibson was in the same habit. Although we are told that at this point there was laughter, we are not told what sort of laughter it was; perhaps it was of a nervous kind or perhaps of a polite nature which comes from embarrassed listeners trying to ease a difficult moment. Indeed, it may have been a little ungracious of Houfton to rub salt into the wound but for reasons which are not clear (but are reminiscent of the first opening ceremony) he seemed to have strong feelings about this matter. Once the point had been made, he continued at length. This, he asserted, would be a railway which would serve an important district; both in mineral wealth and population, now and in the future. He was of the opinion that although a great deal was being said about Doncaster (no doubt a reference to the GNR and also the developing South Yorkshire coalfield), the mineral wealth of the area served by the Mansfield Railway would be greater and he looked forward to it serving the developing coalfield in East Nottinghamshire. He reminded his audience of the difficulties they had encountered in construction because of the war. When the line was begun in September 1911, it was anticipated three years would see it completed. Not so, although part of the line had opened in 1913 between Clipstone Junction and Mansfield Colliery. He went on to outline the various stages in the opening sequence leading up to the completion which they had gathered to celebrate. He regretted that at present there could only be five passenger trains and speculated that had the Government's war-time restrictions not prevented it, there could well have been 20.

The speech continued, as Houfton displayed a determination to milk the opportunity to make his views known. He laboured the fact that the war had made it extremely difficult to find men to carry out the work. He then became fired, it seems, with great emotion, even becoming melodramatic in a manner reminiscent of the great Victorian speeches of the previous century. He did not mind, he asserted, 'if we [the company] suffered if we could help win the war; indeed the line, once finished would help the country to win'. He said he was sure every shareholder was glad the company could do something to win the war. Whether money was made or lost it did not matter considering the cause being fought. (Certainly laughter would have been inappropriate at this point but we are not informed whether there was the nervous shuffling of feet.) Then came what, by any standards, was a most remarkable flourish as he declared

> We must support those brave fellows of ours who have gone out and are fighting so bravely and dying so cheerfully and suffering and enduring with a most magnificent

spirit. We want to see their efforts brought to a successful issue ... All individual matters are nothing, whether engaged in coal, railways or other industries. Empire counts for everything. The overall importance is to win the war.

He might have stopped at that point; the grand finale which would have won him an ovation from those present. But no; there was still more to come. He went on to relate how he had joined a party for dinner at the Swan in Mansfield to meet Directors of the GNR but how it was the enterprise of the Bolsover Colliery Company and the support of the Duke of Portland which had finally made the scheme a reality; of how competition was needed in the Mansfield area. With rather more magnanimity, he stated he did not blame the Midland for what it was doing and felt the GCR or GNR, alone, would have done the same! He then expressed concern about the Government's control of the railway system, suggesting it would have to be modified if continued. Competition was vital, in his view, yet he then argued that state control might well be more beneficial than some systems in the past. Finally (the actual time Houfton was speaking does not appear to be on record) he concluded with the words 'Success to the GCR, who are working the Mansfield Railway'.

Murgatroyd, again for the GCR, was next to rise to his feet. His speech was more moderate and less histrionic than the others. He simply stated that the GCR would do all it could to assist the Mansfield Railway Company; that it would be of great value, bearing in mind the coal traffic; that it would form an important route from South Wales to the East Coast; that the Mansfield company would not be sorry it had chosen to work with the GCR; that although there were indeed only two lines they had been well laid out and that the signalling had been devised to take more traffic, with proper precautions, than any other line of its size in the country. So the gathering ended and another special train took the group back to Mansfield.

Eric Brailsford remembered watching that special train as it arrived back in Mansfield. He was at his grandfather's house in Newton Street and standing in the back yard. A number of people had gathered at the station in Great Central Road to watch and he recalls the smoke box of the locomotive being decked with flags. The locomotive took on water at Mansfield before moving on. In his words:

> The first train was from Nottingham to Ollerton, where the distinguished guests, shareholders and executives had lunch at the Hop Pole. I forgot at what time they came back but a whole lot of people gathered in Great Central Road. I saw it all from grandad's back yard. The engine carried an array of flags on the smoke box and the train stopped in the station and filled up with water.

With the railway now open along the whole of its length, expectations were high. The new route was five miles shorter between Grimsby and London than existing routes and there were now direct dock facilities at Immingham. In addition, the journey to the Dukeries would be made easier. Even so, it was the coal traffic that mattered most. Mansfield, Rufford and Clipstone collieries would be very profitable; the yearly output at Mansfield Colliery was already 1.2 million tons and it was anticipated that the enterprising Bolsover Colliery

Company would exceed this at Rufford and Clipstone given that Clipstone was not yet open. There was also the prospect that Welbeck Colliery would produce a figure approaching one million tons and a further colliery on Lord Savile's Estate adjoining Rufford would be successful. Collieries at Farnsfield and Blidworth were also in the offing. The future looked promising. Coal, the most important commodity as far as the railway was concerned, was, however, not the only one. Mansfield sand was renowned for its use in foundry moulds (there used to be a story that it was exported to Egypt where the sand was unsuitable for making the moulds used in casting!) and it was reckoned this would form an important part of the traffic. The new line was in the care of Mr Lobley, the district inspector at Langwith Junction as it was in his area. The first station master at Mansfield was Mr Bachelor and his assistant, a Newcastle man, was Mr Parkinson.

Once the railways of Britain had been put under Government control, following the outbreak of war, the procedure was to agree a shareholders' dividend based on performance prior to the commencement of hostilities. It has already been seen that there was an anomaly as far as the Mansfield Railway was concerned because the line was only partly open when the war started. Any attempt to base the dividend on the prevailing company conditions at that time was resisted and, arguably, rightly so. In January 1917 the Government had offered the company 4 per cent but this was turned down as unrealistic because a figure of 6 per cent was felt to be more appropriate. In the meantime, the company's Bill to raise further capital had been deposited on 16th December, 1916 and on 2nd February, 1917 the shareholders approved the move at a special meeting. The contractors' retention was also a matter for consideration, following the completion on 4th September of the previous year. However, issues were to arise from this.

It was agreed that the provision of gas at Kirkby-in-Ashfield station should be extended to the signal box at a cost of £76. In connection with the move to obtain new borrowing powers, the GCR agreed to ease the company's financial burden by allowing the accounts of £2,793 2s. 5d., for permanent way materials, to stand over until more money was available. Traffic receipts had resulted in the GCR paying the company £4,622 1s. 7d. To facilitate the easy passage of the Bill, a clause relating to powers to enter into agreements with neighbouring collieries was taken out lest it should attract opposition and so the Bill was passed to the House of Lords. It was hoped it would become an Act by Easter. On 4th April the bank informed the company that it was willing to provide a loan of £40,000, given that new borrowing powers should be forthcoming, and there was an advance of £10,000.

On 27th April, the annual meeting of the shareholders was held. A dividend of 5¼ per cent was announced but it was reported that coal traffic during the initial period had fallen, for the simple reason that the export trade was heavily restricted by the war. Latterly there had been a small increase in traffic. Fair progress had been made with the Rufford branch but there were still problems caused by the shortage of man-power. Progress had also been made with the Concentration Sidings and the western curve beyond Clipstone was nearing completion. The branch to Clipstone Colliery was complete. Capital

ANOTHER OPENING CEREMONY, 1917-1923

expenditure during the half-year had been £26,313, total expenditure up to December (1916) £532,385. Company receipts for traffic had been £1,622. The sinking of Clipstone Colliery was progressing only slowly and there seemed little hope of better progress, again for reasons relating to the war. An area 2½ miles east of Rufford had been found to have a satisfactory top-hard seam of coal and this had been leased. Hopes were expressed that after the war the railway might be extended to develop this coalfield. It was, perhaps, surprising that the new passenger service should terminate at Ollerton, even though connections from there would be available and on 25th May an open letter was written to the company suggesting that it was not proper for the service to end at Ollerton but that it should go through to Lincoln. (A comparison was made with the inconvenience caused if the service terminated at Hucknall instead of going on to Nottingham.) In addition a request was made for a halt to be installed at Forest Town but at a cost of £1,410, the company did not feel it to be justified. A minor irritation had occurred shortly after the opening when signals at Clipstone were tampered with by youths. It was decided that the GCR should liaise with the military authorities in readiness for the introduction of the special trains to the camp at Clipstone.

Traffic did begin to pick up as the year progressed with through traffic carrying steel from Lincolnshire, Admiralty coal from South Wales and, considered to be particularly significant, the fish from Grimsby. The fact that coal could not be exported was lamented when the Board speculated about what might have been possible. Work continued throughout the year on the Rufford branch and the Concentration Sidings and the prospect of the western curve at Clipstone being finished gave the Directors encouragement, given the possibility of getting access to the coalfields along the line from Chesterfield to Lincoln, with the new Welbeck Colliery a particular objective. There was also the potential for a good link to Sheffield and beyond. On 24th May the Bill to raise further capital received the Royal Assent. Meanwhile, the GCR asked for an extension to the telephone and telegraph system with the proviso that it would carry out the work and this proposal was accepted by the company. Matters relating to the accommodation of station masters had to be resolved. These involved a proposal to build a station master's house at Sutton-in-Ashfield and tenders were invited. Somewhat to the surprise of the Board, only one tender was received, this being for £1,290 which was considered to be too high. In December, after further deliberations, the Directors decided not to go ahead with the scheme to build. For Kirkby-in-Ashfield, it was agreed that two houses on The Hill belonging to the company should be altered and adapted but the tenants refused to move out. It took a magistrate's order and several months to remove them before work could be started in December. At Mansfield, the station master, Mr Bachelor, was called to military service and a temporary appointment was made. He was charged a rent of £20. The signal box at Mansfield was linked by telephone to the shunter's cabin in the goods yard and an electric bell installed at the station to be worked from the signal box. At Rufford Junction the starting signals had to be electrically indicated and this work was carried out by the GCR.

As mentioned previously, by September it was reported that the Clipstone Camp branch was virtually ready to carry passengers but the service, introduced on 1st October, was deemed inadequate. In view of this it was decided that from 1st January, 1918 an additional train should run each way between the camp and Nottingham. The Board of Trade had informed the company that two trap points must be put in place on the branch and the Railway Signal Co. Ltd carried out this work, together with the fitting of a fog signalling machine at Kirkby, again at the request of the Board of Trade. By now the western curve was complete and the signal box built, although needing the installation of equipment and this, it was reckoned, would be in place by the end of January. The Board of Trade was notified regarding the carrying of passengers, whilst the GCR had already made plans to use it for freight. On a less demanding level, Newgate Lane School in Mansfield approached the company to ask whether it might have the use of a small piece of land adjoining the school and owned but not needed by the railway, for 'cultivation purposes'. Strangely, perhaps, the Board felt it needed to defer making a decision!

Passenger traffic

The Mansfield Railway operated a passenger service for what, in comparison with other lines, must seem a very short period; a mere 38 years. Nevertheless, it saw not only local trains, running between Nottingham, Mansfield and, at various times, Edwinstowe and Ollerton, but, because of its strategic position in relation to the GCR system, long distance services which passed over the branch and in many cases did not simply use it as a route, but stopped as well.

Given that when the railway opened, England was at war, this factor considerably influenced the pattern of passenger services. It will be recalled that Houfton, at the opening ceremony, expressed disappointment that only five trains a day would be possible. However, soon there were, in addition, special trains provided for the army camp at Clipstone which was the largest camp of its type during World War I. Once this war was over, services improved markedly.

The first services were announced in the local press in March, ready for the opening on the 2nd April, 1917. The timetable reads as follows:

Up trains		am	pm	pm	pm	pm
Ollerton	dep.	9.10	–	–	7.10	–
Edwinstowe	dep.	9.15	–	–	7.15	–
Mansfield	dep.	9.32	1.00	3.20	7.32	9.55
Sutton-in-Ashfield	dep.	9.40	1.08	3.28	7.40	10.03
Kirkby-in-Ashfield	dep.	9.46	1.14	3.34	7.46	10.09
Hucknall	dep.	9.58	1.25	3.45	7.57	10.20
Bulwell	dep.	10.03	1.30	3.50	8.02	10.25
New Basford	dep.	10.07	1.34	–	–	–
Nottingham	arr.	10.12	1.39	3.56	8.08	10.31

Down trains		am	am/pm	pm	pm	pm
Nottingham	dep.	7.30	11.48	2.05	5.46	8.55
Bulwell	dep.	7.38	11.56	2.13	–	9.03
Hucknall	dep.	7.44	12.02	2.19	–	9.09
Kirkby-in-Ashfield	dep.	7.58	12.16	2.33	6.10	9.23
Sutton-in-Ashfield	dep.	8.04	12.22	2.39	6.16	9.29
Mansfield	arr.	8.12	12.30	2.47	6.24	9.37
	dep.	8.15	–	–	6.26	–
Edwinstowe	dep.	8.30	–	–	6.41	–
Ollerton	arr.	8.34	–	–	6.45	–

1918 – *The Rufford branch is completed*

The year 1918 started well for the company. On 1st January, it was able to take over the Concentration Sidings from the contractors. This was seen as an important step as the facility to store and marshall wagons became available. These sidings were sometimes referred at the outset as 'The Duke of Portland's Sidings' (Railway Clearing House map of 1923, *see page 6*). This early designation may have been an acknowledgement of the Duke's support for the project. However, it seems the name was soon dropped. Further, not only was the western curve ready for use also the branch to Rufford Colliery was complete. This section, again perhaps in deference for his support, was originally referred to as 'Lord Savile's Siding' (Railway Clearing House map of 1923). There was, however something of a sting in the tail. The contractors were 108 weeks in arrears with the branch and, further, the western curve and Concentration Sidings were 95 weeks in arrears and Clipstone Colliery branch was 56 weeks in arrears. The company felt there was no option but to apply penalty clauses. Colonel Pringle passed the western curve for use on 19th February. The Board of Trade informed the company that it required a branch near Bleak Hills for the purpose of hauling timber. The company's Engineer was asked to supervise the work which would be paid for by the Government. This line was to connect to a narrow gauge line built by a Canadian Army unit to carry timber from Caudwell Wood. It seems that in the event this branch was not built but there were, until quite recently, still traces of the narrow gauge railway. Elliott-Cooper was to suffer personal tragedy, in March, when it was reported that his son, Lieutenant Colonel Neville Bowes Elliott-Cooper VC, DSO, MC had died after being wounded in action. The company, meanwhile, decided to pursue the matter of the penalty relating to the arrears and put in a claim to the contractors for £25,900. By June the camp branch was very much in use and it was reported that 42,000 personnel had passed over it during April. The Concentration Sidings were also very busy, so much so that the GCR requested additional telephone communication. The Directors inspected the Rufford Colliery branch on 6th June and on 8th July it saw the first traffic, although some signalling levers needed modifying. In spite of the penalty claim, final certificates for Contracts 1 and 2 were issued on 18th July. Mansfield, Clipstone (which would not open fully until 1922) and Rufford collieries were now provided with rail links. Next on the schedule came Blidworth.

Copy

R 4561/17
MANSFIELD RAILWAY No.2

Railway Department
Board of Trade
26 Abingdon Street, S.W.1

18th. December 1918.

SIR,

I have the honour to report, for the information of the Board of Trade, that, at the request of the Company, I made an inspection, on the 13th. instant, of Railway No. 2, authorised by the Mansfield Railway Act, 1914.

This branch line commences at Rufford Junction and terminates at Clipstone Colliery Empty Sidings. The total length of single line is 45.63 chains. At the termination of the Branch the Clipstone Camp Military Railway commences.

The permanent way on Railway No. 2 consists of secondhand 86lb single head rails, in 30ft lengths, laid on 50lb cast-iron chairs, which are supported on transverse sleepers of the usual dimensions, twelve to the rail-length.

There is one brick-arched under-bridge with a span of 12 ft.

The steepest gradient is 1-75 and the sharpest curve has a radius of 8 chains.

Railway No. 2 is to be worked by one engine in steam carrying a staff. An intermediate connection leading to the Colliery Full Sidings is worked from a 2-lever ground frame controlled by the key on the staff. At the terminus the junction with the Military Railway and the siding connections to the Colliery are controlled from a ground frame with 9 levers, of which one is spare. The interlocking in these two frames is correct.

There are no distant signals; but, in view of the fact that the speed over this railway is restricted to 10 miles an hour, I do not consider them necessary.

Railway No.2 was intended as a Colliery line; but, in order to meet Military requirements, passenger working has been adopted between Rufford Junction and Clipstone Camp platform, which is separated by a distance of 200 or 300 yards from the Empty Sidings ground frame at the terminus of Railway No.2. A separate staff is used over the Military Line between the Empty Sidings ground frame and the Camp platform. The connections at the Military platform are worked from a 5-lever groundframe, controlled in some cases by the key on the engine staff and in others by a special key.

The Military portion of this line was not submitted for inspection; but as passengers are booked in the ordinary routine to and from Clipstone Camp, and there is no arrangement for detraining them at the terminus of Railway No. 2 I thought it advisable to look at the working arrangements at the passenger terminus. I think these may be accepted as meeting the requirements in a case of this description where the speed is restricted to 10 miles an hour.

I recommend the Board to approve Railway No. 2 under the Mansfield Act, 1914, for passenger working in the manner and at the speed described.

I have the honour to be,
Sir,
Your obedient servant
(Signed) J.W.Pringle

Further schemes and another Bill

The Newstead Colliery Co. approached the Mansfield Railway Co. with a view to constructing a line to this new colliery at Blidworth. The railway company readily responded but decided to go further. It was anticipated Bilsthorpe would soon have a colliery and so it seemed sensible to include a scheme for a rail link there, in the same Bill to be put before Parliament. In the event the situation did not prove as simple as the Directors had hoped. On 23rd October the Chairman and Deputy Chairman became a committee with full powers to act in advancing the plans to build these two branches. This Bill, which was again drawn up by the same solicitors who had drawn up the previous ones, is dated 11th November, 1918. It seeks approval to construct two further branches (*see map overleaf*). Railway No. 1 was the Bilsthorpe branch, a distance of 3 miles and 1 furlong. This would leave the Rufford branch near Elmsley Lodge. Railway No. 2 was the Blidworth branch, a distance of 2 miles 1 furlong and 3 chains. This would also leave the Rufford branch and both lines would be laid, to a very considerable extent, on land belonging to Lord Savile. The Bill also sought powers to raise further capital. On 17th December the Bill was deposited with an estimated cost of £75,052 for the work. It was unopposed at this stage. In December it was announced that 'Lord Savile's Siding is now being used by traffic'. Some of the inhabitants of Clipstone presented the Board with a memorial (petition) for a halt at Clipstone (mentioned earlier) and it was decided to give this consideration at a future meeting. The Bill now went on to the House of Lords.

There had been discussions with the Midland Railway about the possibility of jointly constructing a branch to Bilsthorpe but in January the Midland decided against this and the Mansfield Railway Co. minuted that 'owing to the expense of directing the traffic for this branch they were compelled to give up the idea of sharing with us the expense of construction and that they will probably make their own connection to the colliery from Farnsfield'. Southwell Urban District Council raised objections to the Mansfield Railway Bill on several counts. These included the proposed span of the bridge over the Nottingham and Ollerton Road and the level crossing on the Eakring Road. For the former, the company had planned a span of 25 ft but the council insisted the span should be 57 ft with a headway of 15 ft 6 in. The Engineer was prepared to settle for 35 ft with a 15 ft headway but the council then proposed a span of 45 ft. The Board, however, was not prepared to increase beyond 35 ft. The level crossing proved to be impractical anyway and the line was taken under the road.

On 13th December Colonel Pringle revisited to inspect Railway No. 2 as authorized by the 1914 Act (the branch to Clipstone Colliery). This visit was in connection with the fact that although normally a mineral line, this section was being used by the War Office for troop movements. He noted that the branch would be worked by one engine in steam carrying a staff. He was happy with the fact that there were no distant signals, given a speed restriction of 10 mph. Colonel Pringle concluded that he could recommend the approval for passenger working.

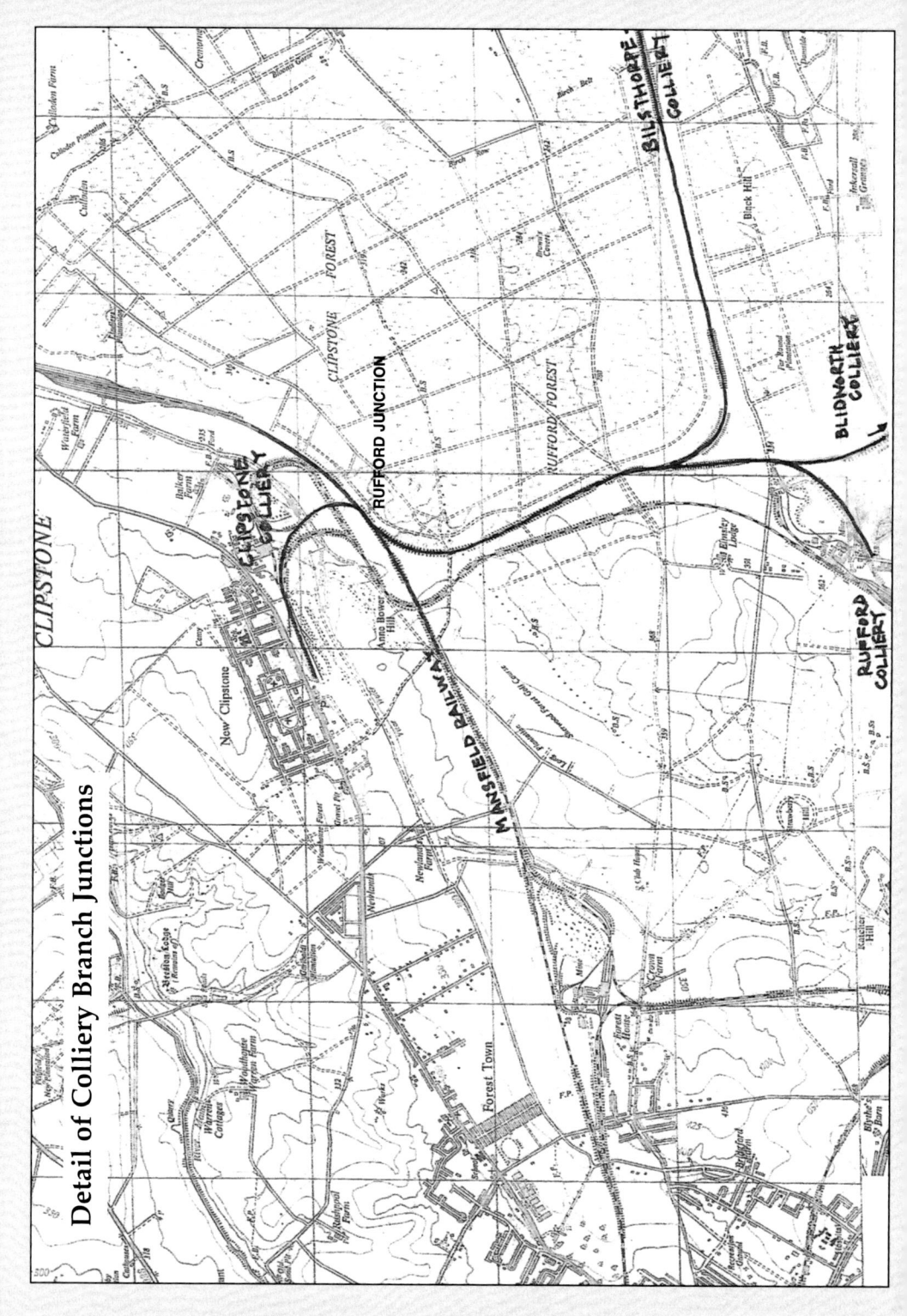

Detail of Colliery Branch Junctions

A postcard view of Blidworth Colliery. *Author's Collection*

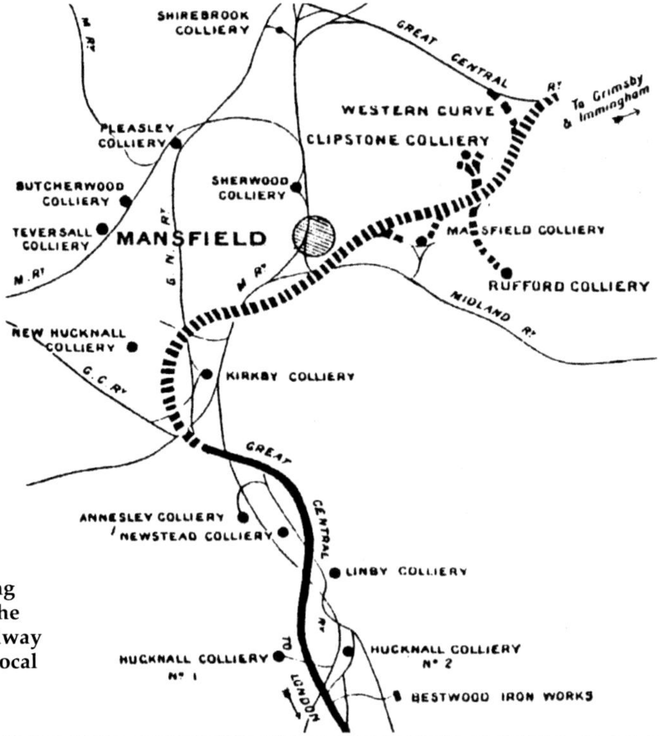

Plan showing position of the Mansfield Railway in relation to local collieries

The first GCR timetable

The GCR timetable of 1918 is the first one issued by the GCR which gave details of services on the Mansfield Railway. Two more trains were introduced in this year. Trains from Nottingham left at 7.37 am (for Ollerton), 9.40 and 11.48 am (for Mansfield and the army camp), 1.40 pm (for Ollerton), 4.40 pm (for Mansfield), 5.46 pm (for Ollerton), 8.55 pm (for Mansfield) and on Saturdays only, 10.35 pm (for Mansfield). Up trains left Ollerton at 9.13 am, 2.58 pm and 7.10 pm; from the army camp at 11.25 am and 1.40 pm and Mansfield at 5.42 pm (this train stopped at all stations including Hucknall, Bulwell Hall Halt, Bulwell Common, New Basford and Carrington). There was a train from Mansfield at 9.55 pm (except Saturdays) and one on Saturdays only at 10.10 pm. Journey times were: Nottingham to Mansfield, approximately 40 minutes; Mansfield to Ollerton, approximately 20 minutes.

From the outset there appeared to be an assumption that the line was owned by the Great Central Railway and not the Mansfield Railway Co. There seem to be various factors which resulted in the widespread colloquial use of the term 'The Central' when speaking of the line and this continued long after the Great Central had ceased to be the operator and to the time (and in some cases beyond) when passenger services ended.

There appear to be a number of reasons for this. Perhaps because the road on which the station in Mansfield stood was named 'Great Central Road' or because it was Great Central locomotives and stock that operated on the line, The most likely reason could well be that the names of the stations carried the word 'Central' in their titles; Mansfield Central (to distinguish it from Mansfield Town on the Midland line), Sutton-in-Ashfield Central and Kirkby-in-Ashfield Central, to clarify to which of the stations in these places reference was being made.

1919 – Some opposition and change of plan

On 16th February the Bill mooted during the previous year was considered by the Lord Chairman's Committee which agreed it should proceed. There were now three petitions against it and these came from Nottinghamshire County Council, Southwell Rural District Council and Stanton Ironworks Co. Ltd. The first two were still concerned about bridge spans and the third took issue with the rates. The hope was expressed that these matters could be resolved to remove the petition. At this point it was decided to remove Railway No. 1 (the Bilsthorpe branch) from the scheme and Bill. As a result the latter went forward unopposed. Amidst all this activity Elliott-Cooper received a knighthood. The decision to remove Railway No. 1 from the scheme meant that the capital powers being sought dropped from £100,000 to £60,000.

A threat appears

A threat which now loomed for the company involved the proposals to build an extension to the Mansfield & District Light Railway (a tram system) as far as Clipstone. The system had already reached Crown Farm (*see map page 62*) and it was reckoned that the scheme, if realized, would take 90 per cent of the passenger traffic for Clipstone Camp. On 7th May there was a local inquiry and the commissioners intimated that they would be prepared to limit the extension to Forest Town provided an adequate service was established.

The Act – A setback and a further plan

In July the Mansfield Bill received the Royal Assent and became an Act. The Newstead Colliery Co. was informed but came back with the news that it was not yet ready to progress its plans. It seems the proposal for a branch to Bilsthorpe was far from defunct and in September it came up again with the Stanton Ironworks Co. expressing the desire to have the line made, either by Parliamentary powers or by private arrangement with the landowners, in order to connect the colliery with the Rufford branch. In fact the proposed scheme was very similar to the one dropped from the previous Bill. In October, Stanton Ironworks confirmed plans for a line to Bilsthorpe Colliery and undertook to pay the costs. The Mansfield Railway Co. was prepared to accept this but with a proviso that the company would have the right to purchase, at cost, within a 20 year period should it be needed for access to other collieries. Other issues with which the Directors had to deal in this period included the situation at the Concentration Sidings near Clipstone. These were continuing to handle a considerable amount of traffic but the company was concerned about the use of the sidings for traffic which did not actually use its line and therefore gain revenue for the company. Sir Sam Fay when approached about this, proposed the GCR should pay 2*d*. per ton and this was accepted. However, the company did make the point that it was not prepared to extend the sidings simply for the purpose of dealing with this type of traffic. C. Clough & Co., wagon repairers, asked the company for a siding at the Mansfield goods yard to further their business and was ready to pay the cost of £410 for this facility. The Board accepted this proposal and, further, a rent of £45 per annum was settled. The dispute about the contractors' settlement had not been resolved and on 4th November, Houfton, Craven and Sanders, together with Elliott-Cooper, met at 15 Deans Yard, Westminster, to discuss the matter. They then adjourned to Browns Hotel and were joined by Pilling and also Baldrey and Yerburgh, who represented the contractors. The latter claimed £35,405 11*s*. 6*d*. was still owing to them. After an initial discussion, the contractors withdrew (as had Elliott-Cooper) and the Mansfield Railway group decided the claim should not be entertained and that, if necessary, arbitration must be sought. The contractors then offered to remove a claim for interest on the amount which stood at £1,140. The company felt it still could not agree and, at this point, decided the offensive was the better stance and persisted in pursuing the counter claim previously made.

At the end of 1919 the Directors asked the Secretary to undertake a comparison with passenger numbers travelling on their line and that of the Midland, given the Midland was running twice as many trains. The encouraging result was that the bookings per train were heavier than the Midland. In some ways this was probably not surprising. The Mansfield stations of both companies were not in the centre of the town and there was quite a steep climb up to the Midland station. In Nottingham, the Midland station was well removed from the city centre whereas the GCR's Victoria station was close to the city centre. These factors remained a consideration for travellers right down to the end of the period when a choice existed.

In 1919, the army camp was still very much in use and there were few changes. The timetable gives three trains from Nottingham which ran through to Ollerton, four trains to Mansfield with two through to the camp, three from Mansfield to the camp by way of connections with two further trains from Mansfield to the camp on Saturdays. Trains from Nottingham were scheduled to stop at Bulwell Common, Hucknall Town (with one exception), Kirkby-in-Ashfield and Sutton-in-Ashfield before reaching Mansfield. They then went on to Edwinstowe or Ollerton. The first train of the day ran as follows:

Nottingham	dep.	7.37 am
Bulwell	dep.	7.45 am
Hucknall	dep.	7.51 am

then on to the Mansfield Railway

Kirkby	dep.	8.04 am
Sutton	dep.	8.09 am
Mansfield	arr.	8.15 am
	dep.	8.18 am

then after leaving the Mansfield Railway

Edwinstowe	dep.	8.33 am
Ollerton	arr.	8.37 am

This journey time was typical for this service.

The camp shuttle left Mansfield at 8.30 am and reached the camp 12 minutes later at 8.42 am. Further trains left Nottingham at 9.40, 11.48 am, 1.40 and 4.40 pm. The last train through to Ollerton left Nottingham at 5.49 pm with the final train of the day leaving Nottingham at 8.56 pm, arriving and terminating at Mansfield at 9.34 pm. Again, there was a connection for the camp with this train.

There were three trains leaving Ollerton for Nottingham daily at 9.11 am, 2.56 and 7.08 pm. Trains from the camp made connections at Mansfield: trains left there at 9.33 am (ex-Ollerton at 9.11 am) 11.23 am, 1.40, 3.18 pm (ex-Ollerton at 2.56 pm) 5.40, 7.30 pm (ex-Ollerton at 7.08 pm) and 10.10 pm. Three of these trains called at Bulwell Hall Halt: the 1.40 and 5.40 pm ex-Mansfield and the 4.40 pm ex-Nottingham.

It was, as mentioned previously, a source of complaint from the outset that trains terminated at Ollerton instead of going through to Lincoln. Later, trains would terminate at Edwinstowe, the first station on the ex-LD&ECR, and connections would be provided there for Ollerton and beyond. There were no Sunday trains in this period.

Holiday and excursions trains

The coming of the railways in the 19th century had brought about, in many ways, a marked change in social patterns. Although the advent of the Mansfield Railway post-dated what was nothing short of this major transition, there were still ways in which it could influence these developing patterns. One of the most obvious aspects was the opening up to more people of the family outing ; the excursion and the family seaside holiday. Once the distressing memories and experiences of the Great War had started to recede, England had entered upon a new and, for some, a very exuberant era. It was as if the former horrors had to be redressed by a period of frivolity and fun. The 'Roaring Twenties', as they became known, were years renowned for hedonistic attitudes which, in many ways, very much displayed the opposite of those during the war. Family life was also something many began to enjoy again and even for those who did not have the means to indulge in fripperies, there was a desire to pursue leisure activities, especially in the form of outings. Opportunities were seized to meet this need in a way that only the railways could do so, at that time.

The Mansfield Railway became part of the plan, as Dean and Dawson of Boar Lane, in Leeds, became instrumental in arranging a large number of excursions in conjunction with the GCR. In 1922, for example, they advertised a number of options. There was the possibility of having six or eight days away travelling by train from Mansfield at 2.30 pm on Monday 12th June for Leicester, Rugby, Aylesbury, High Wycombe and Marylebone. Every Friday during the summer season it was possible to travel to the West of England and South Wales and every Saturday to the places named previously and, in addition, the South of England, the Isle of Wight and the Channel Islands. For those with a taste for horse racing there were day trips to Ascot and these trains, which left at 7.50 am, included a dining car. In fact, Dean and Dawson continued to arrange 'specials' after the demise of the Mansfield Railway and the GCR and following the inception of the LNER. Football specials became a particular feature with cheap tickets available from Mansfield and other stations on the line to a variety of venues during the football season. These were operated throughout the 1920s.

1920

Negotiations relating to the Bilsthorpe branch hit a problem early in 1920. The GCR had said that it would support the plan for Stanton Ironworks to effect a junction with the Mansfield Railway provided it (the GCR) could have an undertaking to work the branch in perpetuity. The Stanton Company was not too sure about this. On another front, there was falling revenue as far as the camp traffic was concerned and the Ministry of Transport then exercised powers to increase these rates. The GCR was asked to consider a bonded warehouse in the neighbourhood of the Old Vicarage in Mansfield. The group dealing with the contractors' dispute met at the Midland Grand Hotel, Saint Pancras, on 20th February, and a decision was made to offer the contractors £23,615 9s. 9d.; this figure to include all items and no further payment would be considered. In April the contractors made another counter claim of £26,500 and at this point a final settlement of £25,000 was agreed.

A lengthy agreement was eventually drawn up on 6th February to enable Mr C. Clough to set up a business as a railway wagon builder and repairer near Mansfield. Clough clearly needed access to the Railway and various conditions relating to this had to be agreed.

There were often misgivings by the railway companies during this period of Government control, especially with small companies such as the Mansfield Railway. The manner in which the Government seemed reluctant to hand back the railways to their Boards gave rise to suspicion in some quarters about the Government's motives and real intentions. The Chairman expressed some concern in July 1920. This related to the comparatively small amount of coal passing over the line compared with the total output of the collieries along the line. As a result, the solicitor was instructed to question the matter of claims from the Government. Another issue raised at about the same time concerned the shareholders' half-yearly meetings. The Secretary suggested that these should be discontinued and there should be annual meetings. The Board accepted this and agreed to hold an AGM in either March or April. At this point, a proposal to construct a platform at Clipstone for workmen's trains was put forward and the GCR agreed to run four trains each way daily with a fare structure as follows: 6½d. per day, 3s. 3d. per week of six days and 3s. 9½d. for seven days. However, there had to be a guaranteed minimum of £75 per week to make the scheme financially viable. No capital outlay was needed for this development and the company stood to gain £1,560 per annum as its portion of the income. This plan to build the platform for workmen's trains foundered and was put in abeyance following a decision by the colliery to seek to purchase the camp station and use this for these trains.

When the Board met on 9th December, there was further concern expressed about the future of the railways and the moves being made by the Ministry of Transport. As Government plans for the future of Britain's railways were pushed ahead, this concern continued to grow. One important aspect involved questions about the distinctions between the owning and working companies; in this case the Mansfield Railway and GCR respectively. The issue was whether original working agreements should be modified in the light of the Government's scheme to acknowledge the need for large increases in rates to meet working expenses and the fact that these expenses were borne solely by the working company and not by the owning one. Under the original agreement the Mansfield Railway was taking a portion of the monies intended, it was argued, for working expenses. The Mansfield Railway engaged counsel to act on its behalf and meantime awaited a report from the Advisory Rates Committee.

1921

In March 1921 the matter had not been resolved and the GCR pointed out to the Mansfield Railway that the Ministry of Transport might object to it (the Mansfield Railway) receiving its full share of the gross receipts under the working agreement on the grounds just outlined, namely, that the increase in rates and charges were intended to meet increased expenditure and therefore not to be divided between the working and owning companies. The Secretary had taken the opinion of counsel as to whether the company would be justified in distributing, by way of dividends or otherwise, the profits of the year as shown in the accounts. Counsel informed the company that the GCR and Ministry of Transport were bound by the terms of the working agreement as drawn up by the GCR and Mansfield Railway so the latter was entitled to a proportion of the gross receipts according to that agreement. The Ministry of Transport was not ready to accept this, however, and a letter from the General Manager of the GCR was sent to the Mansfield Railway, pointing out that the Ministry of Transport had objected to the GCR paying over the full amount due to the Mansfield Railway; the share of the gross receipts for the half year ending 31st December, 1920. As a result, the GCR only paid over £10,000 instead of £16,457 11s. 11d. which the Mansfield Railway expected to receive. Counsel was asked to pursue the matter and in the interim the accounts were annotated with the comment 'The payment of the dividends is subject to adjustment of accounts with the Minister of Transport'. In June (1921) it was reported that the amount payable to the company by way of compensation for loss of traffic was agreed at £12,543 16s. 1d. for the period ending 31st December, 1920 and £14,134 13s. 7d. for the period up to August 1921 This was paid over by the GCR but because the company's plea was upheld the figure of £6,457 11s. 11d., which had been withheld for traffic receipts for the half year ending 31st December, 1920 was also paid. Sanders suggested that in view of the Government's moves it might be better to approach the GCR to settle terms of purchase rather than wait for the Act and the Board asked him to speak with Sir Sam Fay about this possibility. Negotiations continued throughout the year.

When the annual ordinary general meeting was held on Wednesday 8th June, 1921, Houfton made a lengthy comment on the precarious nature of the situation relating to all small railway companies in relation to the large ones, given the way things appeared to be moving. Clearly he had their company and GCR very much in mind. He felt the statutory rights of the small companies were under fire and there was 'a distinct attack upon the sanctity of Parliamentary agreements'. He obviously felt very strongly about this and the way in which the small companies were being, as he seemed to imply, shabbily treated. He went on to make a rather unusual remark given the circumstances.

> If the sanctity of a parliamentary agreement is once laid open to attack it will be impossible to raise money in future for the promotion of small railway companies such as our own. These companies have been of the utmost value to the country and while the traders and districts which the railways serve have, as a rule, benefited very largely from the enterprise of promoters in very few instances have the shareholders of such railways yet reaped the full reward for their venture.

He also reflected on the way in which their company had been seriously disadvantaged by its position when World War I started, commenting,

> We have in the Mansfield Railway a property which has great possibilities and but for the war we should now have been enjoying a very large revenue from our enterprise. One eminent railway authority has stated in his opinion this is a 10 per cent line and your directors will use their best endeavour to try and obtain due protection for the shareholders in the passage of the Bill through Parliament.

1922 – The Government makes known its plans for Britain's railways

The proposals for the Blidworth Colliery branch had come to the fore again in March 1922. Powers for compulsory purchase would expire in July but under Special Acts (Extension of Time) 1915 and Ministry of Transport Act 1919, the Ministry had been empowered to grant extensions of 12 months and it was resolved that application should be made for this. The licence for Mansfield station refreshment room was also about to expire and this was re-awarded for a further five years. The request to make a halt at Forest Town was supported by the GCR because the company argued it would be profitable. However, the Mansfield Board did not feel that at this point the £2,000 could be justified. Fay's suggestion that a loading dock should be provided at Sutton was approved, the cost to be £327. In addition, a facility was made at the Mansfield siding to allow oil to be run off into tank vehicles; the cost to be £30.

By this time the Government's intention for the railways had become apparent. It planned to bring together all the nation's railway companies into four main groups. The Mansfield Railway was destined to be in what was being referred to as 'the North Eastern amalgamation'. In April it was reported that there had been no progress with the plans for this absorption. As if all this was not enough, the GCR was having problems with the Mansfield refreshment room. There had been heavy losses! The GCR asked for a reduction in rent to £10 per annum, to be backdated to the previous 1st January. As the Mansfield Railway had only recently renewed the licence, it was not very keen to take this step and deferred a decision. In July the matter was left for the Chairman to deal with and by October he had managed to settle for £20 per annum. In July, also, Chadburn died. He had been with the company from the outset and his fellow Directors expressed their sense of considerable loss. Further discussions regarding the 'absorption' took place in the second half of the year and the Secretary informed the Board that an amount equal to two years fees was being adopted generally by the companies as compensation to the auditors for loss of office and this was accepted. Payment of 1,250 guineas to the solicitors for negotiating, completing and carrying the scheme through was also approved.

There was news of a different sort in late July when Houfton became the MP for East Nottingham. Other rather more mundane matters needed attention. A request had been made for the making of a siding to the gas works and the electricity works and the proposal to widen Baums Lane, in Mansfield, was on the agenda again, the issue being who would bear what portion of the cost. Mansfield Corporation was described as 'being difficult'. The corporation also wanted a siding to its works and a meeting was convened at the town hall to meet representatives of the corporation. Pilling informed them that they must pay the expenses of connection (the GCR had estimated these at £5,300) and, in addition, the maintenance. If these conditions were met, the company would be prepared to work the siding. As part of the deal the corporation agreed to consider the Baums Lane issue. The cost of the work by this time was put at £2,133 against an original figure of £8,710 but the Mansfield Board was asked to increase its contribution. At this point Pilling suggested that the matter be left until after 'the North Eastern amalgamation' (which, in effect, became the LNER), but he did add that in his opinion the original agreement of May 1915 should be honoured.

The GCR timetable for 1922 gives 11 weekday trains leaving Nottingham for the Mansfield line, of these six went through to Ollerton, with a seventh on Saturdays. There were three Saturday or Wednesday only trains.

In outline, the pattern for down trains is given below:

	am	am	am	am	am SO
Nottingham d.	6.45	7.10	8.00	9.40	10.55
Mansfield	7.25	7.48	8.39	10.24	11.23
Ollerton a.	7.40	–	8.54	11.03	–

	am/pm	pm SO	pm	pm a	pm	pm	pm	pm b	pm WSO
Nottingham d.	11.48	1.10	1.40	3.23	4.40	5.46	7.30	8.56	10.35
Mansfield	12.46	1.51	2.20	4.10	5.25	6.25	8.02	9.36	11.12
Ollerton a.			2.39	4.48		6.44		9.52	

a Via Warsop. *b* Continues on to Ollerton on Saturdays only.
SO - Saturdays only, *WSO* - Wednesdays and Saturdays only.

All the trains from Nottingham called at Kirkby-in-Ashfield and Sutton-in-Ashfield with some calling at New Basford, Bulwell Common, Hucknall and Edwinstowe. The pattern for up trains was:

		am	am	am	am a	pm	pm	pm	pm
Ollerton	dep.			9.11	10.23		1.03	1.03	
Mansfield		7.05	8.00	9.33	11.20	12.20	1.25	1.25	2.00
Nottingham	arr.	7.37	8.31	10.13	12.00	1.00	1.58	2.06	2.41

continues		pm	pm	pm	pm	pm	pm SX	pm SO
Ollerton	dep.	3.05			7.08			
Mansfield		3.27	4.25	5.45	7.30	8.25	10.10	10.20
Nottingham	arr.	4.06	5.00	6.31	8.06	9.00	10.46	10.56

a Via Warsop. *SO* - Saturdays only, *SX* - Saturdays excepted.

By this time there was a Sunday service although trains did not run east of Mansfield. Trains left Nottingham at 10.25 am, 12.10, 3.05, 5.53 and 8.02 pm. Departures from Mansfield were at 9.15, 11.02 am, 12.10, 4.25, 6.40 and 9.20 pm.

In June of this year it was announced that Mansfield would be linked to London (Marylebone) by a new through service with a journey time of just under three hours. The schedule was,

Mansfield	dep.	8.12 *am*
Sutton-in-Ashfield	dep.	8.19 *am*
Kirkby-in-Ashfield	dep.	8.24 *am*
Nottingham	dep.	8.45 *am*
London Marylebone	arr.	11.10 *am*

A restaurant car was provided on this train. The return service left Marylebone at 4.55, reaching Mansfield at 7.54 pm. In fact there was already, at this time, a through 'express' from Mansfield to Marylebone and this was re-timed to leave Mansfield at 7.05 am and arrive at Marylebone at 10.36 am. The train was complemented by one which left London at 4.30 pm but terminated at Nottingham, where a change had to be made for Mansfield.

1923

In February 1923, Sanders, the Mansfield Secretary, informed Lord Faringdon (the Deputy Chairman of the LNER Directors) that the terms for the absorption were inadequate and suggested the matter should go to tribunal. Meanwhile the sinking of Blidworth Colliery had commenced and Sanders contacted the LNER to give them details. As for the plans for absorption, lengthy negotiations followed. On 26th April, 1923 the chief legal advisor to the LNER reported that no agreement had been reached and therefore the case would come before the Railway Amalgamation Tribunal. The date was fixed for 14th May. However it would seem that further negotiations took place. On 16th May Sanders wrote to Faringdon,

After my interview with you, yesterday, I understand the offer is: The LNER will:

take over:	The GCR debt of £25,549 18s. 7d. and the bank loan of £38,966 8s. 1d. £120,000 5% debenture stock of Mansfield Company
give:	£250,000 preferential stock to Mansfield Company's shareholders in exchange for £200,000 5% preference shares
The ordinary shareholders £250,000 5% preferred ordinary stock and £50,000 deferred stock.

The Directors' compensation will be £4,000 (equivalent to four years fees).
Mr Haig Brown and Mr Sanders to be compensated.

Lord Faringdon reported these matters to his Board on 10th May. On 1st June a meeting was held between the two parties and also on 7th June when Houfton had hoped to be present. William Whitelaw (the Chairman of the LNER Directors) took the chair and it was reported that 'on the authority of Lord Faringdon a proxy in favour of J.P. Houfton, whom failing, Thomas Craven for the meeting of Proprietors of the Mansfield Railway Company held on June 1st, to *inter alia*, approve of the terms agreed for absorption had been sealed on 28th May in respect of 2,500 shares formerly held by the Great Central Railway Company'. Other demands appear to have been met, although not all. There is a record that by 21st June the loan (of £39,121 16s. 8d.) which The Mansfield Railway had from the Westminster Bank at Chesterfield had been repaid under the terms of the absorption agreement. (Even later, in February 1924 the LNER was approached by G.S. Herbert & Sons, sharebrokers, asking if the company wished to buy Mansfield 5 per cent redeemable stock. The holders were from Aberdeen, Sussex, Hampshire, Devonshire, Norfolk, Abergavenny and Bolton. On 17th March, the LNER decided against the purchase!)

An AGM was held on 1st June at the Midland Grand Hotel, Saint Pancras with the Board being represented by Houfton, Craven and Knowles. Sanders was present together with a group of shareholders. The last meeting of the Directors of the Board of the Mansfield Railway was also held at the Midland Grand Hotel, on Tuesday 26th June, 1923. Houfton, as always, was in the chair and present were just two others, Craven, still the Deputy Chairman, and Sanders. Sanders reported that on 5th June he had met Faringdon and sorted out the gratuities for the staff and that the LNER had discharged the loan to the Westminster Bank.

The Mansfield Railway, in existence for only 13 years, now became part of the LNER. It had been one of a select group of small companies which had retained its independence from inception to the great amalgamation of 1923. Unlike the cases of some other railways, which were in the same position, there seemed to be no lamenting at the steps being taken. Perhaps it had not been open long enough for a local attachment to develop or possibly because it was not in a comparatively remote rural area where such sentiments might be found. It turned out that there was much more to come. The coalfield it served continued to expand and it was now up to the LNER to make the necessary links, building, as it did, on the sound foundations of the Mansfield Railway Company.

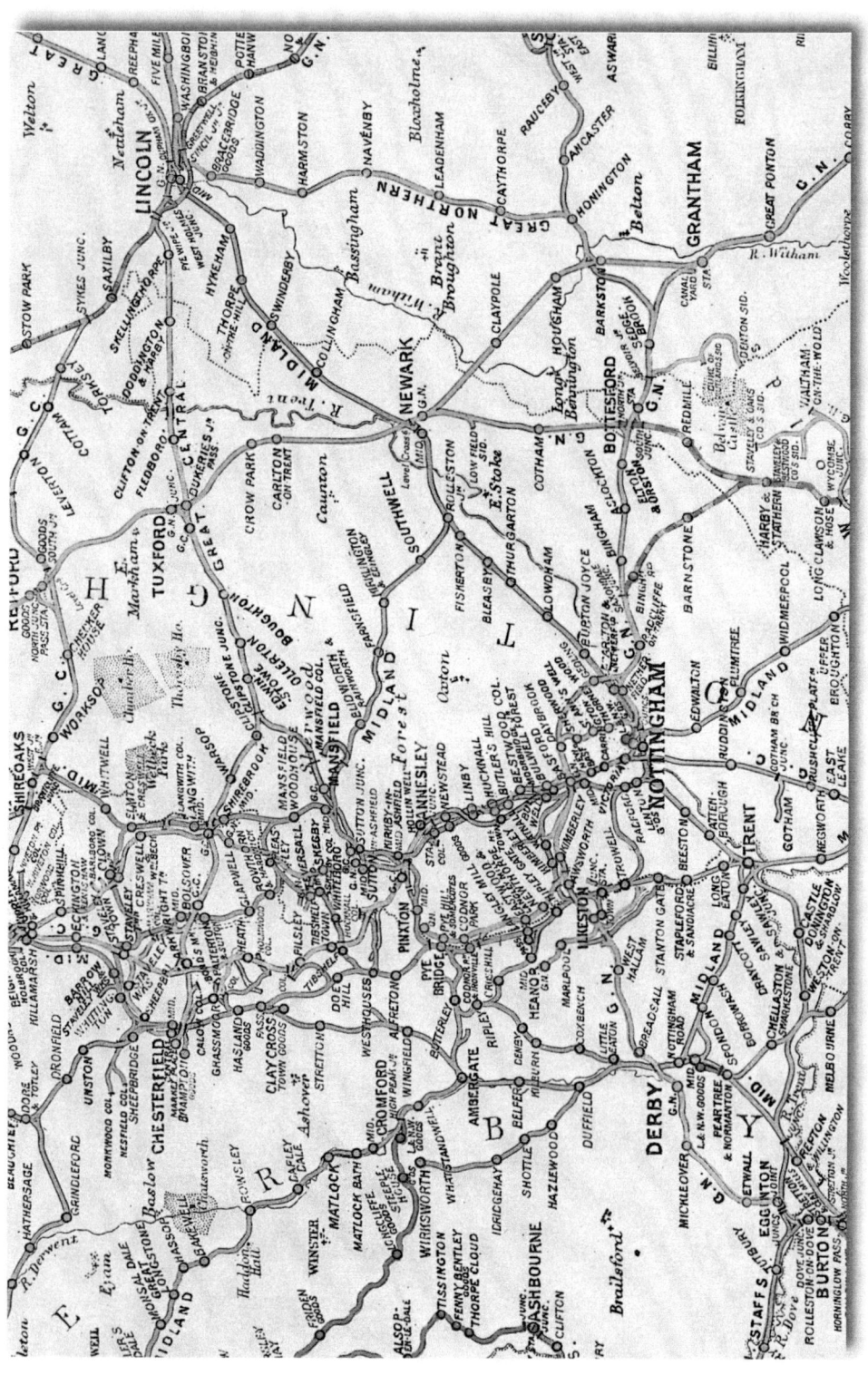

This Railway Clearing House map from 1923 shows the Mansfield Railway and surrounding railways.

Chapter Four

The LNER era, 1923-1947

When the Mansfield Railway became part of the LNER in 1923, the pattern of services remained much as before, with 12 down trains from Nottingham; three going through to Ollerton.

World War II (1939-1945) would bring changes. Once again, coal exports would cease and passenger services would be reduced. After the war it would soon become clear that times were changing. The internal combustion engine was in the ascendancy. Even in the period before the war, bus services were very much on the increase. An indication of growth is shown by the fact that in 1924, 240 'omnibuses' were licensed for use in Mansfield and district and only a year later the number had increased to 408, although of these, 10 were charabancs and 60 were taxis. The companies with the majority of the omnibuses were Trent Motor Traction and Underwoods (later to become the East Midland Company). Bus companies were required to provide proper time-tables to meet the conditions for licensing and so a properly structured service was emerging and eventually this would prove a real threat to rail services. The post-war period would see an even greater growth in bus companies and services.

However, the main development during the initial years of the LNER era was, without doubt, the significant progress in the mining industry. When the LNER took over the Mansfield Railway there was considerable scope for development. Mansfield, Clipstone and Rufford collieries were already being served by the railway but two others, Bilsthorpe and Blidworth looked set to become important sources of revenue.

The Blidworth branch 1923-1934

The Mansfield Railway had obtained powers by the Act of 1919, mentioned previously, to construct a branch to Blidworth Colliery. At that stage, the promoters of this colliery were the Newstead Colliery Co., the Sheepbridge Coal & Iron Co. and the Staveley Coal & Iron Co. Events had led to the Mansfield Railway having to seek a time extension for compulsory purchase orders and this had been granted. The sinking of the colliery was about to begin and it was thought coal would be reached in about three years. At that time the cost of the branch was estimated at £52,000; this figure included the cost of the land. The compulsory purchase powers would expire on 24th July (1923) and so it was deemed necessary to serve notices to treat.* The Board actually authorized the construction of this branch to Blidworth Colliery on 26th January, 1926 and so by this date much of the land needed had been acquired. On 13th December, 1925 it had been reported that Lord Savile's land at Rufford was priced at £1,798, land belonging to S.W. Welfitt at Farnsfield was priced at £70 and at Blidworth, J.H.T. Ruswell's trustees wanted £175 and Sir Charles Hilton Seely, £210. It was noted

---

* Treat is a legal term often used in railway parlance and signifies a formally concluded and ratified agreement for purchase.

the Newstead Colliery Co. was not requiring payment for its land which the railway would need. The total cost was £2,253. The cost of the work was estimated at £78,850, this to include the contribution of £5,500 being half the cost of the shared work at the colliery. The tenders were opened in July 1926 and covered a considerable range. The highest came from Monk & Newall at £112,041 with a construction period of 30 months; the lowest was from H. Arnold at £53,937 with a 12 to 15 month completion period. The latter tender was accepted. The largest single cost was the viaduct over the LMS line from Mansfield to Southwell, east of Rainworth. This would be £3,709. The LNER had to pay an easement of £50 to take the branch over the LMS line at this point. There had also been protracted negotiations with the LMS in connection with that company's intention to serve the colliery. The discussions had been over the matter of shared facilities at the colliery itself and the outcome was an arrangement that the running road and the loop to the empty wagon sidings and the necessary signal box and signalling would be constructed and maintained at joint equal cost of the LMS and LNER. There would also be equal rights of ownership on this section. It was proposed that the LNER branch would commence with a branch from the Rufford Colliery branch and terminate by a junction with the joint running road to the sidings, just described. The Newstead Colliery Company, which was responsible for the actual sinking and operating of the colliery, would pay for further siding accommodation for loaded and empty wagons. It was reckoned that 3,000 tons of coal would be moved daily and the LNER share of the traffic had a projected income of £53,125 per annum.

There had been rapid progress with the sinking of the colliery and by 13th January, 1926, a top hard seam 3 ft 7 in. had been reached in No. 2 Shaft at a depth of 721 yards. The Union Jack was flown to mark this significant event and there was something of a sense of relief. The reason for this was that it had not been deemed necessary to make any trial holes before the 'sinkers', used to make the shaft, had been put to work. The boring had gone considerably deeper than that needed at neighbouring mines and there were those who started to doubt whether coal would be reached. However, reached it eventually was, in No. 2 Shaft. No. 1 Shaft, which had reached 677 yards, had to be taken deeper. By this time the LMS had practically completed its branch to the colliery. Work on the LNER scheme was started and proceeded well. Certainly no problems had been anticipated in the actual construction work but another of a different nature arose. The work was nearing completion in August 1928 with only ballasting and signalling (at a cost of £6,674) being needed, when the Newstead Colliery Company announced that the mine would close 'for an indefinite period'. The reason given, on 22nd August, was that the depression in trade made it inappropriate to remain open and the contractors were requested to terminate their work. This obviously came as a great blow. The expenses to that point had been £56,327 and the total was expected to be £63,000 (nearly £16,000 less that the original figure). The problem was what to do next! The work on the railway was discontinued pending a further decision by the colliery company but it was some time before this came.

In the meantime, discussions took place about arrangements if the colliery did reopen. In January 1931 the traffic committee of the LNER proposed that the colliery company should forward 50 per cent of the competitive traffic by its company, in addition to all local LNER traffic. The colliery company was not prepared to accept this and protracted negotiations followed. In the end the clause 'reasonable share' of the competitive traffic plus LNER local traffic was agreed. 'Reasonable share' was not, however, defined clearly. In September 1932 the colliery company intimated that it would re-open the mine although it was anticipated output, certainly initially, would be small. At this stage the colliery company questioned the wisdom of completing the branch. However, as production rose and an output of 250,000 tons per annum was achieved, the LNER reckoned that as there was very little work to be done to finish the line and a considerable quantity of this coal could be destined for places on its system and beyond, the time was right and completion was effected. This was done in the first half of 1934.

The Bilsthorpe branch

The early problems associated with the plans to provide Bilsthorpe Colliery with a rail link have also been mentioned already and the LNER re-examined this situation on taking over the Mansfield Railway. It was noted that on 13th December, 1923 powers were being sought by the company in a Bill to construct a line about three miles long from the Rufford Branch to Bilsthorpe and that a temporary line would be constructed to assist with the sinking. In an agreement of 28th August, 1924, the railway company gave an undertaking that as soon as coal had been proved to exist, it would construct a permanent railway and aim to complete this by the time coal had been reached and was being mined. The Stanton Ironworks Co. anticipated that this would be in June 1927 (although this proved to be over optimistic) and gave the following projections on output:

		Tons per day
1927	June to September	400
	October to December	1,000
1928	January to June	1,500
	July to December	2,000
1929	January to June	3,000
	July to December	4,000

The British Empire Exhibition

In 1924/25 the British Empire Exhibition was held in London. Dean & Dawson, the company which operated tours and visits, offered the people of Mansfield and district the possibility of visiting this illustrious event. There were options of one day, four day or eight day visits to London which included a chance to visit the exhibition. The dates for travelling up to London were 3rd, 10th, 17th, 24th, and 31st, October, 1925. The train, run by the LNER, picked up at Shirebrook North (6.45 am) followed by Warsop (6.50) Mansfield LNE (7.10) Sutton Central (7.20) Kirkby Central (7.25) Hucknall Central (7.40) and thence

No. 1083

A DAY AT THE SEASIDE.

Wednesday, 2nd September.

DEAN & DAWSON'S THROUGH DAY EXCURSION

WILL RUN TO

SKEGNESS

AS UNDER:

FROM	Times of Departure.	RETURN FARES Third Class.
	a.m.	s. d.
LEICESTER (Central)	7 20	} 10 0
LOUGHBORO'	7 35	
NOTTINGHAM (Vic.)	7 55	
KIRKBY-IN-A. (Central)	8 20	} 9 3
SUTTON-IN-A. (Central)	8 25	
MANSFIELD (L.N.E.)	8 30	
SKEGNESS .... arr.	10 43	

Passengers return same day only from Skegness at 8.45 p.m.

Children under Three years of age, Free; Three and under Twelve, Half-fare.

The tickets are not transferable, and are issued upon the condition that they are available only on the dates and by the trains in each direction mentioned in this bill, and for the stations named upon them, and if used by any other trains than those herein mentioned, or to or from any station short of or beyond that to which they are available, they will be forfeited, and Full Ordinary Fares charged.

The Company gives notice that tickets for this excursion are issued at a reduced rate, and subject to the condition that the Company shall not be liable for any loss, damage, injury or delay to passengers arising from any cause whatever.

NO LUGGAGE ALLOWED.

Passengers are requested to obtain their Tickets in Advance.

Tickets and Bills can be obtained any time in advance at the Company's Booking Offices and Stations; **The Company's Office, 22, Clumber Street, Nottingham;** also from **Messrs. Dean & Dawson's, 1, Gallowtree Gate, Leicester;** and **3, Upper Parliament Street, Nottingham; Messrs. King & Bird, Leeming Street, Mansfield;** and the usual Agents.

For further information apply to **District Manager, Nottingham (Vic.),** or the **Passenger Manager, Liverpool Street Station, London, E.C. 2.**

LONDON, AUGUST, 1925.   (Via Lincoln.)   H & S Ltd.

For a Programme of Holiday Tours, write to or call at Dean & Dawson's Offices.

on to Wembley Hill (the nearest station to the exhibition and one which had been specially refurbished) the arrival time being 10.49 am and Marylebone at 11.05 am. Third class day return fares ranged from 13s. 6d. from Shirebrook to 12s. 6d. from Hucknall. The price for four or eight days ranged from 23s. 6d. to 21s. 6d. Shirebrook to Hucknall respectively. The price from Mansfield was 22s. 9d. (The cost of entry to the Exhibition was not included in the train fare and was 1s. 6d. for adults and 9d. for children.) For those in Nottinghamshire who wanted to visit this remarkable exhibition, the only practical way to travel there was by train.

The Mid-Notts Joint Railway

There was also a plan to gain access to the collieries from the Mid-Notts Joint Railway for which Parliamentary powers had been obtained but it was anticipated contracts for this scheme would not be placed before May or June (1927) and then the line would take between two and three years to build. The Mid-Notts Joint Railway, as the name implies, was a joint enterprise. The scheme involved the LMS and LNER companies and was authorized in 1926. The line was intended to serve collieries which it was envisaged would open in the vicinity of Calverton and also Bothamsall. The line was planned to run from Bestwood Park Junction, south of Hucknall, to Farnsfield and Ollerton and then join the line between Worksop and Retford at the northern end. As it turned out, only part of the line was built, this being the middle section between Farnsfield and Ollerton. It is reported that the LNER ran very few trains over this middle section of the Mid-Notts. A colliery was not built at Bothamsall although much later one was sunk at Bevercotes and the 'northern' section of the line was modified somewhat to serve it.

1925-1926

By January 1925 the temporary line to Bilsthorpe Colliery had been constructed at a cost of £17,400 (£2,875 being paid to Lord Savile for 32½ acres of land) with the colliery company paying five per cent per annum on the cost until a permanent railway was completed. It was also agreed that the colliery company would refund to the railway company the cost of any portion of the temporary line which could not be absorbed into the permanent line. The railway company would also negotiate for the purchase of land for the permanent railway. In September 1926, a matter of some urgency arose when the colliery company announced that coal might be mined by September the following year. The cost of the permanent line had been estimated as £61,930 although the LNER revised this to £59,200. Tenders were invited and at a meeting of the works committee at Marylebone station on 28th October, the tenders were opened and ranged from £95,767 12s. 4d. from Monk and Newall to £49,790 13s. 3d. from H. Arnold & Son. The contract was awarded to H. Arnold & Son but their tender was later revised to £41,689 after an error had

No. 1124

British Empire Exhibition at Wembley.

INTERNATIONAL SHOE AND LEATHER FAIR, October 5th to 9th	ROYAL
DAIRY SHOW .... October 20th to 23rd	AGRICULTURAL
BREWERS' EXHIBITION .... Oct. 31st to Nov. 6th	HALL.
MOTOR SHOW .... October 8th to 17th	AT
COMMERCIAL MOTOR TRANSPORT EXHIBITION, Oct. 29th to Nov. 7th	OLYMPIA.

On Saturdays, 3rd, 10th, 17th, 24th and 31st October, 1925
(for 1, 4 or 8 days).

Dean & Dawson's Excursions will run to

WEMBLEY HILL
(NEAREST STATION TO EXHIBITION)
and
LONDON (Marylebone)

AS UNDER :—

		Return Fares—Third Class	
FROM	Times of Departure.	To Wembley Hill and Marylebone Day.	To Marylebone only 4 or 8 Days
	a.m.		
Shirebrook North (for Langwith)	6 45	13/6	23/6
Warsop	6 50	13/0	23/3
Mansfield (L.N.E.)	7 10	13/0	22/9
Sutton-in-Ashfield (Cen.) ..	7 20	13/0	22/9
Kirkby-in-Ashfield (Cen.) ..	7 25	13/0	22/0
Hucknall (Cen.)	7 40	12/6	21/6
Wembley Hill .. arr.	10 49		
London (Marylebone) .. ,,	11 5		

Passengers holding Excursion Tickets travelling by trains calling at Wembley Hill (the nearest station to the Exhibition) will be allowed to break the journey at that station and travel forward to Marylebone later in the day, if they so desire, without extra charge, joining the return excursion at Marylebone.

Passengers holding DAY Excursion Tickets only travelling direct to Marylebone will be entitled to travel to Wembley and back without extra charge.

A FREQUENT SERVICE OF NON-STOP TRAINS WILL RUN BETWEEN MARYLEBONE AND THE EXHIBITION STATION (inside the Ground, adjoining the India Pavilion), by which these tickets will be available.

Admission Tickets to the British Empire Exhibition can be obtained on application to any office of Dean & Dawson, Ltd.

WEEK-END TICKETS (First and Third Class) at about **a Fare and a Third** are issued to any station as under :—

ON FRIDAYS { By any train at or after 12-0 noon and before 5-0 p.m. MINIMUM FARE: **15/-** Third Class.
{ By any train at or after 5-0 p.m. MINIMUM FARE: **10/-** Third Class.
ON SATURDAYS—By any train. MINIMUM FARE: **5/-** Third Class.
AVAILABLE FOR RETURN ON FOLLOWING SUNDAY....By any train after 6-0 a.m.
ON FOLLOWING MONDAY....By any train.

For a Programme of Holiday Tours write to or call at Dean and Dawson's Offices.

been found when adding up the amounts of various sections! Completion time was set at 15 months with the contractors maintaining the line for 12 months after opening. A clause in the contract made it clear that no passes or privilege tickets would be issued and that the contractors' men would be required to pay full fares in going to and from the works. There were no difficult sections and the only two items involving some considerable cost were an over-bridge over the Bilsthorpe Road (£2,899) and a bridge over the Nottingham Road (£3,547 16s).

1927

Coal was reached by August (1927) and Bilsthorpe was able to claim having the most up-to-date colliery in the country. There were two shafts, each 20 ft in diameter and 500 yds deep, with these shafts being lined with concrete down to a depth of 300 yds, necessary because the ground was so wet. Electricity was generated on site by mixed pressure steam turbines each generating 1500 kilowatts. Although coal was being mined by the beginning of September, some work was incomplete. The screening and washing plants were only partly operational and the pit-head baths had not been finished.

Bilsthorpe was the last of the collieries to be built which would be served by the 'Mansfield Railway' and with the completion of the Bilsthorpe branch, the whole system was complete.

The colliery branches used the key token system, with key token instruments at Bilsthorpe Junction and Blidworth Junction (for Blidworth and Rufford collieries) and the LNER issued special instructions for Rufford and Bilsthorpe collieries. On the Rufford branch, the section of the empty line between the points leading to the empty wagon sidings and the buffers would accommodate no more than 30 wagons. The procedure, therefore, if there were more empty wagons than this on a train arriving, was for the guard to secure the train first and then divide it on the running line. The guard was also to ensure that the trolley lines crossing the empty siding were not in use. Loaded wagons had to be propelled from the 'loaded' sidings to the loop at a speed not in excess of 3 mph and the guard was instructed to walk alongside the leading wagon. Detailed instructions were also given for dealing with a train of empties arriving at Bilsthorpe and the subsequent removal of loaded wagons. On the arrival of a train of empty wagons at the 'empty wagon reception' sidings, which were immediately to the west of Bilsthorpe Road bridge, the engine was to be uncoupled and run round the train so that it could move the wagons to the colliery company's empty wagon sidings. However, before this movement could start, the shunter on duty at Bilsthorpe had to obtain permission, by telephone, from the colliery Empty Weigh Office and then accompany the train so that the points could be set at the sidings for whichever siding was to be used for the train. Once this permission had been given, the colliery company staff at the sidings were instructed to cease all movements until the (LNER) engine and brake van had left the siding. The brake van then had to be left on the branch to the empty wagon sidings and the locomotive proceeded to pick up loaded

L·N·E·R
THE NEW ROUTE TO THE
MIDLANDS, SOUTHAMPTON
AND
BOURNEMOUTH
THROUGH EXPRESS
(RESTAURANT CARS FROM NOTTINGHAM)

WEEK-DAYS, Commencing 11th JULY.

		a.m.
Leeds (Central)	Dep.	10. 0
Holbeck	,,	10. 3
Wakefield (Westgate)	,,	10.22
Doncaster (Central)	,,	10.50
Retford	,,	11.13
Mansfield (L.N.E)	,,	11.49
		p.m.
Nottingham (Vic.)	Arr.	12.31
Leicester (Central)	,,	1. 7
Rugby (Central)	,,	1.41
Oxford	,,	2.53
Reading (West)	,,	3.39
Southampton (Terminus)	,,	5.39
,, (West)	,,	5. 9
Bournemouth (Central)	,,	6.13
,, (West)	,,	6.28

Similar through train in reverse direction leaves Bournemouth (West) 11.2 a.m.; Bournemouth (Central) 11.13 a.m.; Southampton (Terminus) 11.35 a.m.; and Southampton (West) 12.11 p.m.

TOURIST AND WEEK-END TICKETS ISSUED.

Seats reserved on application to Station Master's Office, Central Station, Leeds, L·N·E·R Office, 141, Briggate, or Messrs. Dean & Dawson, Ltd., 51, Boar Lane, Leeds.

L·N·E·R
DEAN & DAWSON'S
Summer Holiday Excursions
From MANSFIELD (L.N.E.R.)

EVERY FRIDAY, for 8 and 15 Days.
TO

SOUTH AND WEST OF ENGLAND, ISLE OF WIGHT, CHANNEL ISLANDS.—Bournemouth, Portsmouth, Southampton, Banbury, Bath, Bristol, Dawlish, Devonport, Exeter, Falmouth, Penzance, Plymouth, St. Ives, Swindon, Taunton, Torquay, Ilfracombe, Looe, &c.

SOUTH WALES.—Aberdare, Abertillery, Barry, Bridgend, Cardiff, Merthyr, Newport, Swansea, &c.

IRELAND.—Belfast and Dublin.

EVERY SATURDAY, for 8 and 15 Days.
TO
LONDON (Marylebone).

SOUTH OF ENGLAND, ISLE OF WIGHT, CHANNEL ISLANDS.—Bexhill, Bognor, Bournemouth, Brighton, Deal, Dover, Eastbourne, Folkestone, Hastings, Margate, Portsmouth, Ramsgate, St. Leonards, Southampton, Westgate, Whitstable, Worthing, &c.

EASTERN COUNTIES.—Beccles, Bungay, Bury St Edmunds, Cambridge, Clacton, Colchester, Cromer, Felixstowe, Harwich, Hunstanton, Ipswich, Lowestoft, Norwich, Sheringham, Wisbech, Yarmouth, &c.

MIDLANDS.—Leicester, Rugby, Stratford-on-Avon, Aylesbury, High Wycombe, Princes Risborough.

LINCOLNSHIRE.—Lincoln, Grimsby Docks, Cleethorpes, Skegness, Sutton-on-Sea, Mablethorpe, &c.

YORKSHIRE.—Barnsley, Bradford, Doncaster, Halifax, Huddersfield, Hull, Mexborough, Penistone, Rotherham, Goole, &c.

LANCASHIRE.—Liverpool, Manchester, Oldham, St. Helens, Southport, Warrington, Wigan, Blackpool, &c.

wagons. Once these had been collected, the locomotive moved forward until the last wagon was clear of the points leading to the branch to the empty sidings, the guard lowered the brake on to the train and once this had been done the train went forward to the Mansfield Concentration Sidings.

J.P. Houfton

What should not pass without mention is that in 1929, during the period when all this was happening, J.P. Houfton died. He had had an enormous influence on events surrounding the making of the Mansfield Railway. He was, as previously mentioned, the Chairman of the Bolsover Colliery Company and one who saw the pressing need to develop the railway system in the area to move the coal from the collieries of that enterprise. He remained Chairman of the Mansfield Railway throughout its time as an independent company, before it become part of the LNER. He had held the offices of Mayor of Mansfield and High Sheriff of Nottinghamshire. There was also his Parliamentary career as the Member of Parliament for East Nottingham. In 1928 he received a knighthood.

The completed line described

At the western end of the line, the Mansfield Railway left the GCR line on the up side, just beyond Kirkby South Junction which is where the GNR Leen Valley line diverged. (Both were under the control of the same signal box.) The line rose on a gradient of 1 in 126. It crossed the Pye bridge and Pinxton section of the Midland and then, by means of a bridge, the GNR curve from the Leen Valley to the GCR, which by this time was no longer in use. The bridge span was later removed and the gap infilled. The first station encountered was Kirkby-in-Ashfield station which consisted of two fairly basic platforms and the station building. There was also a cattle dock and sidings. In later years coaches were housed in the latter on Saturdays in readiness for excursion trains which started at Kirkby on Sundays. The station was in a cutting and this provided an opportunity for landscaping. The floral displays are especially remembered by those who travelled the line. These displays were of such a high standard that they won prizes; in particular first prize in the station gardens competition on several occasions. The man responsible for this work was Bill Brownhill (apparently known to his 'Toc H' friends as 'Chuffer') who was the station clerk. His achievements were even more remarkable because he had only one arm.

After Kirkby, there was a long brick retaining wall on one side and on the other, a masonry wall, both made necessary by the nature of the terrain along this whole section and which had given rise to some problems during construction. These problems arose because it appears trial bores had indicated hard rock but when excavations started it was found to be marl on a bed of sand some six feet deep. The walls were needed to contain this material and had to be made nine feet thick in places. The line then passed through a short tunnel under the Midland Sutton

Town branch. This tunnel may have been unique because the Midland branch whilst crossing the Mansfield Railway was itself crossed by a road bridge close to the same point with the approach roads, so necessitating a tunnel for the bottom line. The cutting virtually extended to the next station, Sutton-in-Ashfield, which was identical in style to Kirkby but with the main building on the up side with a small building on the down side which housed a ladies room and a general waiting room. Beyond Sutton there was a goods yard with four sidings, one for the purpose of unloading coal.

At this point the line started to swing round to a north-easterly direction and was carried on an embankment and then entered a rock cutting. At Bleak Hills dam it was felt necessary to re-enforce the base with stone in order to prevent erosion. The gradient between Sutton and Mansfield was severe with the climb in the up direction resulting in the heavy coal trains, which were travelling westwards, sometimes getting into difficulties and requiring help. During the day this assistance would be provided by the Mansfield station pilot and at night, by the pilot at the Mansfield Concentration Sidings. The line now reached the edge of Mansfield, first passing under the Midland line to Southwell and then crossing the main road from Mansfield to Nottingham on a substantial skew bridge. Beyond this bridge and to the right was Mansfield goods yard. Beyond this the railway crossed the Littleworth road on another skew bridge and entered Mansfield station.

This station stood on what became known as Great Central Road which was formerly a track of little consequence before the arrival of the railway. Quite who thought 'Great Central Road' would be an appropriate name for the new road is unknown but it certainly endorsed the notion to those who were not really well acquainted with the facts that from the outset this was the Great Central Railway. It is no exaggeration to say that Mansfield station was a remarkable edifice ('remarkable' being used somewhat euphemistically); some went as far as to say it was without parallel. It was built on steeply falling ground which resulted in the front of the building, on Great Central Road, being four storeys on the road side but only two on the platform side. It had unusual proportions which gave it a long narrow appearance and one which was not particularly aesthetically pleasing. The whole edifice was also not very inviting and facilities, such as the booking office, appeared dark and cramped. The station platforms were of wood and had an air of semi-permanence or a scheme awaiting completion. The down platform was considerably shorter than the up platform. Perhaps the one redeeming feature was the electric lighting.

Beyond the station, the railway was carried over Ratcliffe Gate by a bridge with three arches. The line now turned in a more easterly direction past Newgate Lane School, through a deep cutting and on towards Forest Town on a rising gradient in an easterly direction of 1 in 400 and 1 in 200. Mansfield (Crown Farm) was the first colliery on the line. There was a branch to serve this and just over a mile further, on a descending gradient, a branch for Clipstone Colliery on the down side and also one for Rufford Colliery on the up side. Just to the east of these were the Concentration Sidings.

After a short distance and crossing the road from Mansfield to Ollerton, at the side of the 'Dog and Duck' public house, the line joined the former LD&ECR (by the time of opening the GCR) with connections east and west. The line had little to boast as far as scenic beauty was concerned. There was a pleasing, if limited, view of the Dukeries when approaching the point beyond Clipstone where the line joined the former LD&ECR line but the really scenic area came beyond this line, when approaching Edwinstowe and beyond.

The colliery branches were just that and served no other purpose. The Rufford branch left the main line, as just described, and the Blidworth and Bilsthorpe branches left from this. However had there been the opportunity for passengers to travel these lines the scenery was quite pleasing, skirting as they did, areas of woodland and ones where ling grew, giving a purple carpet at certain times of year. The Bilsthorpe branch passed over the main Nottingham to Ollerton Road at one point and the Blidworth branch was carried over the Rainworth to Farnsfield Road and Midland line by means of a substantial bridge.

There were signal boxes at Kirkby-in-Ashfield Central, Sutton-in-Ashfield Central, Mansfield, Mansfield Colliery Sidings, Rufford Junction and 'Clipstone' (Mansfield) Concentration Sidings, Clipstone West and Clipstone East. Kirkby-in-Ashfield Central was the first signal box to be closed, whilst, latterly, Sutton-in-Ashfield Central box was only open on the day shift.

The period up to nationalization

Once completed the line was able to realize its full potential. Coal output continued to increase and passenger services, over the next decade, reached something of a peak during the period when these were available. There are good reasons for and evidence of this. The recovery of a sense of optimism and the hope of progress was evolving, following the end of World War I. Whilst there were still many unpleasant memories there was a desire to look forward to better times. Coal was still the major fuel and during this decade production reached higher levels. The railways had the job of transporting this coal because there was no real challenge from road transport. The same was also true of passenger transport. The bus companies were certainly making an impression but there were few cars and most people chose to travel by train whether for work and business or days out and, possibly, holidays at the sea-side.

The working timetable for 1927

Although there was the General Strike followed by a miners' dispute in 1926, by 1927 things were getting back to normal. The following working timetable for the Mansfield Railway for July 1927 gives an indication of how busy the line was even though Blidworth and Bilsthorpe collieries were still to become fully operational. It will be seen that as far as passenger services are concerned another new service was introduced which used the Mansfield Railway. This was a weekday service which left Leeds Central at 10.00 am, stopped at Holbeck, Wakefield (Westgate), Doncaster Central and Retford. It eventually took the Mansfield line after passing through Tuxford, calling at Mansfield Central at 11.49 am. The train from Leeds terminated at Nottingham but there were through coaches. These were attached to a Newcastle to Bournemouth train, which included a restaurant car, for Leicester, Rugby, Oxford and Reading. These went on to Southampton and then Bournemouth Central and West, arriving at the latter at 6.28 pm. A reciprocal service left Bournemouth West at 11.02 am. (This service is referred to again in Chapter 6 'Motive Power') This service was withdrawn after 1932.*

Up trains

12.20 am	[MX] Coal train joins line at Clipstone Junction. Arrives at Concentration Sidings 12.23 am. Destined for Guide Bridge.
1.59 am	[MX] Goods from Immingham to Annesley joins line at Clipstone Junction. Passes Kirkby South Junction 3.10 am.
2.27 am	[MX] Coal train joins line at Clipstone Junction. Arrives at Concentration Sidings 2.30 am. Destined for Guide Bridge.
3.25 am	[MX] Train of coal empties ex-Tuxford West joins line at Clipstone Junction. Arrives Concentration Sidings 3.30. Leaves 6.05 am for Rufford Colliery. Arrives 6.19 am.
6.29 am	[MO] Train of coal empties ex-Tuxford West joins line at Clipstone Junction. Proceeds directly to Rufford Colliery. Arrives 6.48 am.
6.45 am	Passenger train ex-Shirebrook North joins line at Clipstone Junction. Arrives Mansfield at 6.55 am.
6.57 am	[MX] Goods train ex-Manchester joins line at Clipstone Junction. Arrives Mansfield 7.17 am.
7.05 am	Express Passenger leaves Mansfield for Marylebone. Passes Kirkby South Junction 7.20 am [Sutton-in-Ashfield dep. 7.12 am, Kirkby-in-Ashfield dep. 7.18 am].
7.17 am	[MO] Goods ex-Langwith joins line at Clipstone Junction. Proceeds to Kirkby with stops en route. Arrives 8.38 am.
7.22 am	Goods ex-Tuxford joins line at Clipstone Junction. Proceeds to Mansfield. Arrives 8.02 am.
7.42 am	[MO] Coal train joins line at Clipstone Junction. Arrives 7.46 am. Destined for Guide Bridge.
8.08 am	Express Passenger leaves Mansfield for Marylebone. Passes Kirkby South Junction 8.22 am [Sutton-in-Ashfield dep. 8.15 am, Kirkby-in-Ashfield dep. 8.20 am].
8.08 am	[SX] Train of coal empties ex-Tuxford West joins line at Clipstone Junction. Arrives 8.14 am. To work Clipstone Colliery.
8.15 am	Coal train joins line at Clipstone Junction. Warsop Junction to Woodford. Passes Kirkby South Junction 9.28 am.
8.29 am	Passenger train ex-Chesterfield joins line at Clipstone Junction. Arrives Mansfield 8.39 am.
8.45 am	Train of coal empties ex-Langwith Junction joins line at Clipstone Junction. Arrives at Concentration Sidings 8.50 am.

* It was customary to refer to the line as the 'Central' and the station names usually included this description. However on this working timetable the station at Mansfield is referred to as 'Mansfield New Station'.

SO – Saturdays only, SX – Except Saturday, MO – Mondays only, MX – Except Mondays, R – Runs when required, LE – Light engine, EBV – Engine & brake van.

Up trains (continued)

9.20 am	Passenger train from Ollerton to Nottingham joins line at Clipstone Junction. Passes Kirkby South Junction 9.49 am [Mansfield dep. 9.33 am Sutton-in-Ashfield dep. 9.41 am Kirkby-in-Ashfield dep. 9.47 am].
9.30 am	Train of coal empties leaves Rufford Junction for Rufford Colliery. Arrives 9.45 am.
9.44 am	[MSX] [R] Mineral train joins line at Clipstone Junction. Normanby Park to Banbury. Passes Kirkby South Junction 10.45 am.
10.10 am	Coal train leaves the Concentration Sidings for Annesley. Passes Kirkby South Junction 10.58 am.
10.35 am	[MX] Coal train joins line at Clipstone Junction ex Warsop Junction for Annesley. Passes Kirkby South Junction 12.10 pm [Held back for Leeds express].
11.07 am	Passenger train ex-Warsop joins line at Clipstone Junction for Nottingham. Passes Kirkby South Junction 11.39 am. [Mansfield dep. 11.23 am, Sutton-in-Ashfield dep. 11.31 am, Kirkby-in-Ashfield dep. 11.37 am].
11.14 am	Coal train ex-Welbeck Colliery joins line at Clipstone Junction. Arrives at the Concentration Sidings 11.19 am.
11.39 am	Express Passenger ex-Leeds joins line at Clipstone Junction. Passes Kirkby South Junction 12.04 pm [Mansfield dep. 11.49 am, Sutton-in-Ashfield dep. 11.56 am].
11.57 am	Train of coal empties from Pyewipe joins line at Clipstone Junction. Arrives Concentration Sidings at 12.03 pm.
12.20 pm	[SO] Passenger train leaves Mansfield for Nottingham. Passes Kirkby South Junction 12.36 pm [Sutton-in-Ashfield dep. 12.28pm, Kirkby-in-Ashfield dep. 12.34 pm].
12.40 pm	[SX] Train of coal empties ex-Tuxford West joins the line at Clipstone Junction. Proceeds to Rufford Colliery.
12.42 pm	[SO] Train of coal empties ex-Tuxford West joins the line at Clipstone Junction and proceeds to Rufford.
1.13 pm	Passenger train from Ollerton to Nottingham joins line at Clipstone Junction. Passes Kirkby South Junction 1.42 pm [Mansfield dep. 1.26 pm, Sutton-in-Ashfield dep. 1.33 pm, Kirkby-in-Ashfield dep. 1.39 pm].
1.47 pm	Passenger train from Chesterfield joins line at Clipstone Junction for Mansfield. Arrives at 1.57 pm.
1.58 pm	Train of coal empties ex-Whitmoor Colliery joins line at Clipstone Junction. Proceeds to Annesley.
2.00 pm	[SO] Passenger train leaves Mansfield for Nottingham. Passes Kirkby South Junction 2.16 pm [Sutton-in-Ashfield dep. 2.08 pm, Kirkby-in-Ashfield dep. 2.14 pm].
3.05 pm	[SO] Passenger train from Chesterfield joins line at Clipstone Junction for Mansfield. Arrives 3.17 pm.
3.12 pm	Passenger train from Ollerton to Nottingham joins line at Clipstone Junction. Passes Kirkby South Junction 3.43 pm [Mansfield dep. 3.27 pm, Sutton-in-Ashfield dep. 3.35 pm, Kirkby-in-Ashfield dep. 3.41 pm].
3.23 pm	Mineral train from Barnetby to Banbury joins line at Clipstone Junction. Passes Kirkby South Junction 4.29 pm.
3.55 pm	Train of coal empties ex-Tuxford West joins line at Clipstone Junction. Arrives Concentration Sidings at 4.01 pm.
4.17 pm	[SX] Express Fish from Marshgate to Banbury joins the line at Clipstone Junction. Passes Kirkby South Junction 4.46 pm.

Up trains (continued)

4.25 pm	Passenger train leaves Mansfield for Nottingham. Passes Kirkby South Junction 4.41 pm [Sutton-in-Ashfield dep. 4.33 pm, Kirkby-in-Ashfield dep. 4.39 pm].
4.34 pm	Coal train from Welbeck Colliery joins the line at Clipstone Junction and moves to the Concentration Sidings.
4.50 pm	[MX] Coal train leaves the Concentration Sidings for Woodford. Passes Kirkby South Junction 5.43 pm.
5.45 pm	Passenger train leaves Mansfield Station for Nottingham. Passes Kirkby South Junction 6.01 pm [Sutton-in-Ashfield dep. 5.53 pm, Kirkby-in-Ashfield dep. 5.59 pm].
5.55 pm	[SO] Express Fish from Marshgate to Banbury joins line at Clipstone Junction. Passes Kirkby South Junction 6.24 pm.
5.59 pm	Coal train from Warsop Junction to Woodford joins line at Clipstone Junction. Passes Kirkby South Junction 6.51 pm.
6.00 pm	[SX] Goods for Banbury Junction leaves Mansfield. Passes Kirkby South Junction 6.37 pm.
6.04 pm	Coal train from Warsop Junction joins line at Clipstone Junction and moves to the Concentration Sidings.
6.50 pm	Coal train leaves the Concentration Sidings for Annesley. Passes Kirkby South Junction 8.05 pm.
7.15 pm	Passenger train from Ollerton to Nottingham joins line at Clipstone Junction. Passes Kirkby South Junction 7.46 pm [Mansfield dep. 7.30 pm, Sutton-in-Ashfield dep. 7.38 pm, Kirkby-in-Ashfield dep. 7.44 pm].
7.40 pm	[SO] Passenger train from Warsop to Mansfield joins line at Clipstone Junction.
8.35 pm	Passenger train leaves Mansfield for Nottingham. Passes Kirkby South Junction 8.51 pm [Sutton-in-Ashfield dep. 8.43 pm, Kirkby-in-Ashfield dep. 8.49 pm].
8.42 pm	Express Fish from Grimsby Dock to Banbury joins line at Clipstone Junction. Passes Kirkby South Junction 9.17 pm.
9.03 pm	[SX] Express Fish from Doncaster to Banbury joins line at Clipstone Junction. Passes Kirkby South Junction 9.36 pm.
9.40 pm	[SO] Passenger train leaves Mansfield for Nottingham. Passes Kirkby South Junction 9.56 pm [Sutton-in-Ashfield dep. 9.48 pm, Kirkby-in-Ashfield dep. 9.54 pm].
10.04 pm	[SO] Passenger train from Ollerton to Nottingham joins line at Clipstone Junction. Passes Kirkby South Junction 10.34 pm [Mansfield dep. 10.18 pm, Sutton-in-Ashfield dep. 10.26 pm, Kirkby-in-Ashfield dep. 10.32 pm].
10.10 pm	[SX] Passenger train leaves Mansfield for Nottingham. Passes Kirkby South Junction 10.26 pm [Sutton-in-Ashfield dep. 10.18 pm, Kirkby-in-Ashfield dep. 10.24 pm].
10.35 pm	[SO] Passenger train from Chesterfield to Mansfield joins line at Clipstone Junction.
10.46 pm	Goods from Grimsby to Annesley joins line at Clipstone Junction. Passes Kirkby South Junction 11.46 pm.
11.35 pm	[SO] LE leaves Mansfield. Passes Kirkby South Junction 11.52 pm.
11.40 pm	Mineral train from Normanby Park to Banbury joins line at Clipstone Junction. Passes Kirkby South Junction 12.50 am.
11.56 pm	[SX] Goods from Grimsby to Annesley joins line at Clipstone Junction. Passes Kirkby South Junction 12.56 am.
Sundays	Six passenger trains from Mansfield to Nottingham. Mansfield dep. 9.10,11.20 am, 1.10, 4.25, 6.45, 9.20 pm [No Ollerton service].

THE LNER ERA, 1923-1947

Down trains

1.27 am	[MX] Light engine joins line at Kirkby South Junction. Picks up coal train for Whitemoor at Concentration Sidings. Passes Clipstone Junction at 2.21 am.
1.30 am	[MX] Coal train leaves Concentration Sidings for Guide Bridge. Passes Clipstone Junction at 1.36 am.
3.30 am	[MX] Coal train leaves Concentration Sidings for Guide Bridge. Passes Clipstone Junction at 3.38 am.
3.50 am	[MX] Express Fish empties (Woodford to Grimsby) join line at Kirkby South Junction. Passes Clipstone Junction 4.24 am.
4.05 am	[MO] Express Fish empties (Woodford to Grimsby) join line at Kirkby South Junction. Passes Clipstone Junction 4.39 am.
5.25 am	[R] Coal train leaves Concentration Sidings for Pyewipe West. Passes Clipstone Junction 5.31 am.
6.18 am	Passenger train from Nottingham to Mansfield joins line at Kirkby South Junction. Arrives Mansfield 6.36 am [Kirkby-in-Ashfield dep. 6.22 am, Sutton-in-Ashfield dep. 6.30 am].
6.30 am	[MO] Coal train leaves Concentration Sidings for Guide Bridge. Passes Clipstone Junction 6.36 am.
7.15 am	[MX] Coal train leaves Rufford Junction for Pyewipe West. Passes Clipstone Junction 8.21 am.
7.25 am	Passenger train for Lincoln leaves Mansfield. Passes Clipstone Junction 7.34 am.
7.31 am	Passenger train from Nottingham to Mansfield joins line at Kirkby South Junction. Arrives Mansfield 7.45 am [Kirkby-in-Ashfield dep. 7.34 am, Sutton-in-Ashfield dep. 7.39 am].
8.05 am	[MSX] Goods from Woodford to Grimsby joins line at Kirkby South Junction. Passes Clipstone Junction at 10.01 am.
8.10 am	[R] Coal train leaves Concentration Sidings for Bullcroft Junction. Passes Clipstone Junction 8.16 am.
8.27 am	Passenger train from Nottingham to Ollerton joins line at Kirkby South Junction. Passes Clipstone Junction 8.53 am [Kirkby-in-Ashfield dep. 8.30 am, Sutton-in-Ashfield dep. 8.35 am, Mansfield dep. 8.43 am].
8.28 am	EBV leaves Mansfield for Mansfield Colliery. Arrives 8.35 am.
8.40 am	[MO] Coal train leaves the Concentration Sidings for Guide Bridge. Passes Clipstone Junction 8.46 am.
8.55 am	LE leaves Mansfield for Concentration Sidings. To proceed to Rufford at 9.30 am.
9.00 am	[MO] Goods from Woodford to Grimsby joins line at Kirkby South Junction. Passes Clipstone Junction 11.06 am.
9.05 am	LE from Annesley joins line at Kirkby South Junction. To Concentration Sidings 9.35 am.
9.10 am	[MX] Train of coal empties from Woodford joins line at Kirkby South Junction. To Concentration Sidings 9.40 am.
9.15 am	[MO] Coal train leaves Rufford Colliery for Pyewipe West. Passes Clipstone Junction 11.21 am.
10.09 am	Passenger train to Warsop joins line at Kirkby South Junction. Passes Clipstone Junction 10.35 am [Kirkby-in-Ashfield dep. 10.12 am, Sutton-in-Ashfield dep. 10.17 am, Mansfield dep. 10.25 am].
11.19 am	[SO] Passenger train from Nottingham to Mansfield joins line Kirkby South Junction. Arrives Mansfield 11.33 am [Kirkby-in-Ashfield dep. 11.22 am, Sutton-in-Ashfield dep. 11.27 am].
11.40 am	[SO] Goods from Woodford to Grimsby joins the line at Kirkby South Junction. Passes Clipstone Junction at 1.20 pm.
11.55 am	[MX] Train of coal empties from Woodford joins line at Kirkby South Junction. Proceeds to Concentration Sidings.

Down trains (continued)

12.00 nn	Train of empties leaves Concentration Sidings for Warsop Junction. Passes Clipstone Junction 12.06 pm.
12.17 pm	Passenger train from Nottingham to Ollerton joins line at Kirkby South Junction. Passes Clipstone Junction 12.43 pm [Kirkby-in-Ashfield dep. 12.20 pm, Sutton-in-Ashfield dep. 12.25 pm, Mansfield dep. 12.33 pm].
12.45 pm	Coal train for Tuxford West leaves the Concentration Sidings. Passes Clipstone Junction 12.51 pm.
1.00 pm	[SO] Passenger train leaves Mansfield for train to Chesterfield. Passes Clipstone Junction 1.10 pm.
1.37 pm	[SO] Passenger train from Nottingham to Mansfield joins line at Kirkby South Junction. Arrives Mansfield 1.51 pm [Kirkby-in-Ashfield dep. 1.40 pm, Sutton-in-Ashfield dep. 1.45 pm].
2.06 pm	Passenger train from Nottingham to Ollerton joins line at Kirkby South Junction. Passes Clipstone Junction 2.32 pm [Kirkby-in-Ashfield dep. 2.09 pm, Sutton-in-Ashfield dep. 2.14 pm, Mansfield dep. 2.22 pm].
2.18 pm	Train of fish empties from Banbury to Marshgate joins line at Kirkby South Junction. Passes Clipstone Junction 2.48 pm.
3.06 pm	Coal train leaves Concentration Sidings for Pyewipe Junction. Passes Clipstone Junction 3.12 pm.
3.16 pm	Train of coal empties from Annesley joins line at Kirkby South Junction. Proceeds to Concentration Sidings 4.00 pm [Stops when required at Mansfield Colliery. On Saturdays this train picks up at Mansfield Colliery].
3.20 pm	Coal train leaves Concentration Sidings for Immingham. Passes Clipstone Junction 3.26 pm.
3.51 pm	Passenger train from Nottingham to Mansfield joins line at Kirkby South Junction. Arrives Mansfield 4.05 pm [Kirkby-in-Ashfield dep. 3.54 pm, Sutton-in-Ashfield dep. 3.59 pm].
3.56 pm	[SX] Goods from Annesley to Mansfield joins line at Kirkby South Junction. Arrives Mansfield 5.37 pm.
4.00 pm	Coal train leaves Rufford Colliery for Tuxford West. Passes Clipstone Junction 5.08 pm.
4.05 pm	[MX] Coal train from Annesley joins line at Kirkby South Junction. Proceeds to Concentration Sidings 4.30 pm.
4.10 pm	Passenger train for Chesterfield leaves Mansfield. Passes Clipstone Junction 4.20 pm.
4.30 pm	Coal train from Mansfield Colliery to Tuxford West. Passes Clipstone Junction 8.06 pm [at Concentration Sidings until 8.03 pm].
4.46 pm	[SO] Coal train from Annesley to Grimsby joins line at Kirkby South Junction. Passes Clipstone Junction 6.16 pm.
4.59 pm	Passenger train from Nottingham to Mansfield joins line at Kirkby South Junction. Arrives Mansfield 5.13 pm [Kirkby-in-Ashfield dep. 5.02 pm, Sutton-in-Ashfield dep. 5.07 pm].
5.15 pm	[SO] Goods leaves Mansfield for Ardwick. Passes Clipstone Junction 5.30 pm.
5.15 pm	Express Passenger from Nottingham to Leeds joins line at Kirkby South Junction. Passes Clipstone Junction 5.35 pm [Sutton-in-Ashfield dep. 5.27 pm, Mansfield dep. 5.27 pm].
5.45 pm	Coal train leaves Concentration Sidings for Warsop Junction. Passes Clipstone Junction 5.51 pm.
6.09 pm	Passenger train from Nottingham to Ollerton joins line at Kirkby South Junction. Passes Clipstone Junction 6.35 pm [Kirkby-in-Ashfield dep. 6.12 pm, Sutton-in-Ashfield dep. 6.17pm, Mansfield dep. 6.25 pm].

Down trains (continued)

7.00 pm	[SX] Goods leaves Mansfield for Staveley Town. Passes Clipstone Junction 7.15 pm.
7.19 pm	Train of coal empties leaves Concentration Sidings for Welbeck Colliery. Passes Clipstone Junction 7.25 pm.
7.42 pm	Coal train leaves Concentration Sidings for Tuxford West. Passes Clipstone Junction 7.48 pm
7.53 pm	Express Passenger from Marylebone to Mansfield joins line at Kirkby South Junction. Arrives Mansfield 8.07 pm [Kirkby-in-Ashfield dep. 7.56 pm, Sutton-in-Ashfield dep. 8.01 pm].
8.27 pm	Coal train leaves Concentration Sidings for Tuxford West. Passes Clipstone Junction 8.33 pm.
8.27 pm	[SX] Coal train from Annesley to Grimsby joins line at Kirkby South Junction. Passes Clipstone Junction 10.01 pm.
8.56 pm	[SO] Passenger train from Nottingham to Mansfield joins line at Kirkby South Junction. Arrives Mansfield 9.09 pm [Kirkby-in-Ashfield dep. 8.58 pm, Sutton-in-Ashfield dep. 9.03 pm].
9.16 pm	[SX] Passenger train from Nottingham to Mansfield joins line at Kirkby South Junction. Arrives Mansfield 9.30 pm.
9.16 pm	[SO] Passenger train from Nottingham to Ollerton joins line at Kirkby South Junction. Passes Clipstone Junction 9.49 pm [Kirkby-in-Ashfield dep. 9.19 pm, Sutton-in-Ashfield dep. 9.24 pm, Mansfield dep. 9.32 pm].
9.43 pm	[SO] Passenger train from Mansfield to Chesterfield leaves Mansfield. Passes Clipstone Junction 9.55 pm.
11.13 pm	[SO] Passenger train from Nottingham to Mansfield joins line at Kirkby South Junction. Arrives Mansfield 11.27 pm [Kirkby-in-Ashfield dep. 11.16 pm, Sutton-in-Ashfield dep. 11.21 pm].
11.30 pm	[SO] Passenger train for Bolsover leaves Mansfield. Passes Clipstone Junction 11.45 pm.
Sundays	Five down passenger trains, arriving Mansfield at 11.08 am, 12.57, 3.48, 6.36, 9.04 pm [No service beyond Mansfield].
1.27 am	LE (ex-Annesley) passes Kirkby South Junction. Proceeds to Concentration Sidings. Collects coal train for Whitemoor. Passes Clipstone Junction 2.21 am
8.35 am	LE from Annesley to Mansfield. Passing Kirkby South Junction 8.35 am. Arriving Mansfield 8.50 am.

As can be seen, coal movements predominated and there were goods trains which originated in places such as Immingham and Manchester, mineral trains (one from Normanby Park to Banbury; another from Barnetby to Banbury) and three weekday express 'fishes'; one via Doncaster (Marshgate) to Banbury, one from Grimsby Docks to Banbury and the other, coming via Doncaster, to Banbury. There was good provision for passengers (Ollerton-Mansfield-Nottingham was the mainstay and was, in effect, the line's 'own' service) including a Sunday service as well (but not to/from Ollerton). Other passenger services came onto the line from places including Chesterfield, Warsop and Shirebrook. Then there were the 'Express Passenger' trains from Mansfield to Marylebone. The comparative boom in coal traffic resulted in the Concentration Sidings becoming inadequate with the likelihood of being more so once Blidworth and Bilsthorpe collieries went into full production. It was agreed that a new reception road should be constructed together with 10 new sidings on the down side and a further five on the up side.

In the period between the wars and once it controlled the line, the LNER put on specials which gave people an opportunity to have a day at the seaside. The destinations were predominantly on the East Coast with Skegness being particularly popular. These trains would stop at stations on the Mansfield Railway but came from further afield; places such as Leicester. It was made clear in the publicity that these were strictly day excursions and leaflets produced often included the statement 'No luggage allowed'.

A wrong working?

Mansfield was reckoned to be unusual for the number of signals on the up line; a distant, an outer home, an inner home, a starter and an advanced starter. It seems these could give rise to confusion occasionally, as demonstrated in an incident which occurred in the 1930s and described (in a hand written letter to the author) by J.E. Pollard:

> It was the practice for the last passenger train of the day from Nottingham to be worked by Colwick men. This was because the train terminated at Mansfield and after reaching Mansfield, the engine would run round the train and take the empty stock back to either Basford carriage sidings or Nottingham Victoria. On one occasion, in the darkness, the engine had run round the empty stock and this had been coupled up. The driver saw the starter was off and without looking at the ground signal set off. En route for Sutton the fireman spotted a goods train approaching on the 'inside' and about to overtake.
> 'How long has there been a goods line down here?' he asked the driver.
> 'There isn't' replied the driver
> 'There must be' retorted the fireman, 'because there is a train coming alongside us - and fast!'
> There was a certain amount of alarm when this turned out to be a fully fitted fish train! The driver then realized he was taking the empty stock on the facing road to Sutton. The signal he had observed at Mansfield had been for the fish train and not him. Checking the ground signal would almost certainly have confirmed this.

This account has given rise to a lot of debate and discussion over the years, not least relating to the authenticity or otherwise of the account. John Hitchens gives a masterly analysis:

> Although in 1927 the engine from the last train returned to Annesley, in 1939 the empty coaching stock was taken to New Basford and the engine went on to Nottingham and probably to Colwick. In the summer FO the coaches were worked to Nottingham Victoria to connect with overnight trains to the south. A practice continued at least up to 1960. I recall booking this train at Sutton Central.
> The run round would have to be completed and the points reset before the signalman could accept a train on the up line and the signals pulled off.
> Referring to the station signal diagram the up starter is adjacent to the end of the down platform, this is because the station is on a curve and it gives a clearer sighting to an up train.
> The driver, after waiting for some time may have mistaken this for permission for him to move forward, or the guard may have signalled that all was ready for departure. (A

brake test would have been carried out after coupling up the carriages.) I do not think the train (empty stock) would have moved far before he realized his mistake because he could not miss the fact that his engine had not crossed over the points; keeping straight on would not have resulted in any change in the engines sideways motion. Moving forward the line was track circuited and this would have locked the point leading to the down sidings so that it was only possible to run on the down line. Had he continued, because the signal boxes at Sutton and Kirkby would be switched out, his first crossover was at Kirkby South Junction on the main line and the signalman's record would have highlighted this, resulting in an internal enquiry. There was also a problem at Kirkby South Junction, because there were trap points on the down line to protect any runaways on the falling gradient from fouling the main line.

In the 1950s there was a fish train booked after he had left but the 1939 WTT does not show this; only the 9.40 (passing time at Mansfield) of the Doncaster-Banbury Fish. This continued to run into the 1950s I cannot conceive that this train would be running two hours late. The only explanation for the goods train on the Up line was a diversion which could have come from the ECML from the Dukeries Junction or more likely from the GC main line via the ('Clob and Knocker') Clowne or via Duckmanton. I would have thought that a GC tank locomotive was involved and these were right-hand drive. The down trains ran chimney first and so the up trains were bunker first. (This was the same practice as on the Midland.) It was up hill from Nottingham and running this way reduced the chance of the water level over the firebox running too low, especially as the engine would be working quite hard on certain sections. The driver would have been on the wrong side to observe the guard's signal and to see the signal for the up main or the shunt signal for the crossover points. which explains why he would be on the fireman's side and the fireman being on the driver's side. The express goods remains a mystery.

On reflection, an account of how the GN Leen Valley Extension was blocked was exaggerated because there were several ways for the signalman to move the engine out of the way, but this would have spoilt the tale.

An interesting find was a through goods working from Manchester to Kirkby Central via the Duckmanton Curve. There were only facilities for wagon load traffic at Kirkby Central, although I once came across a working of a cattle train from Aylesbury to Kirkby and Mansfield.

1928

In 1928 the matter of the rates for transporting coal came up again and this was dealt with in the Court of the Railway Rates Tribunal and relating to the Railway Act 1921. This involved the Bolsover Colliery Co. (the applicants) and now the LNER (the respondents). The outcome, in March, was, in effect, that agreed formerly, namely that there would be a minimum 500,000 tons per annum from Mansfield and Clipstone collieries and 250,000 from Rufford colliery and the condition that sixpence per ton and a halfpenny per ton should be applied as before in the Agreements of 1910 and 1916.

A decision was made just before the start of World War II to 'rationalize' somewhat and Sutton Central station was put under the supervision of Sutton Town station (formerly of the GNR) and Kirkby Central was put under Kirkby Bentinck. Although it is not really made clear why these steps were taken there is a suggestion that the LNER saw it as a way of cutting costs.

A sleepy-looking Mansfield (Central) station in August 1935.

(Both) Lens of Sutton Collection

'K3' class 2-6-0 No. 159 at Mansfield (Central) with an up train in August 1935.
A.W. Croughton/Rail Archive Stephenson

World War II 1939-1945

The outbreak of hostilities in 1939 saw a reduction in passenger services, although not a drastic one. From October of that year there were six up trains with the same number of down trains on each weekday with two trains on Sundays. The most significant change was that, even on weekdays, there was no service east of Mansfield. By October 1939, there were trains as follows:

Weekdays	From Nottingham at 6.10 am, 12.55, 2.00, 5.47 6.30 and 9.00 pm
	From Mansfield at 7.15, 8.09, 11.25 am, 1.51, 6.42 and 7.50 pm
Sunday	From Nottingham at 2.00 and 9.00 pm
	From Mansfield at 11.25 am and 6.42 pm

These timings, especially the absence of trains from Nottingham during the middle part of the mornings on weekdays, seem to show a very Nottingham-oriented service, possibly with business rather than shoppers in mind.

In 1940 there was a change of policy and trains once again ran east of Mansfield. There were seven trains in May of that year with two running to Ollerton. One of the up trains was ex-Edwinstowe (at 7.45 am) with a 1.25 pm leaving Ollerton, travelling via Warsop, giving passengers a long wait in Mansfield until the 5.48 pm ex-Mansfield.

The general pattern varied little throughout the war, although by May 1943 the number of weekday trains had fallen to six. However, the Ollerton-Edwinstowe services were maintained.

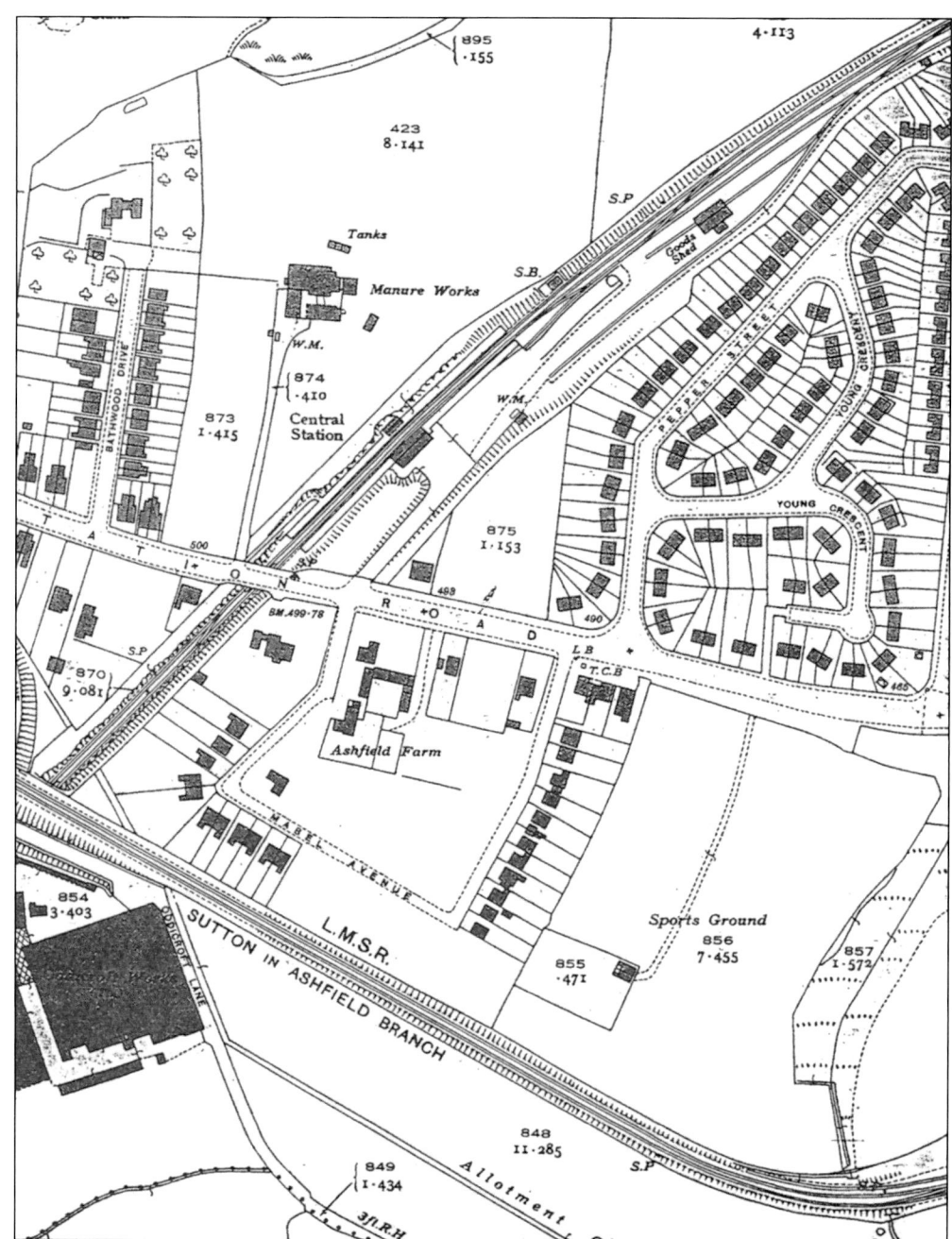

Sutton-in-Ashfield station. Reproduced from the 25" Ordnance Survey map, revised in 1938, published 1947. *Crown Copyright*

Snow

The Mansfield Railway was not usually affected by snow blockages but one such incident was reported in the winter of 1943/44. John Shelbourne, who was studying at University College Nottingham set off to travel back there from Sutton on Sunday 24th February. He recalls that he went to catch the 6.37 pm from Mansfield and expected to arrive at Nottingham Victoria at 7.17 pm. There had been a heavy fall of snow and the train, which would normally have left Sutton at 6.45 pm was considerably delayed, allegedly because points were frozen in the Mansfield area. Eventually, a GCR Atlantic appeared, running tender first and with five coaches in tow. This particular working sometimes had a 'B8' (*Sutton Nelthorpe* had been noted on occasions) and sometimes a 'J39'. The train made very heavy going in the section through the cutting as it travelled towards Kirkby, the wheels slipping frequently. Just beyond the end of the cutting the train came to a halt and stood for two hours. It was, in fact, stuck in the snow and it took four hours before a team from Annesley managed to dig it out. It then advanced slowly to the end of Annesley Yard where the Atlantic was taken off and replaced; probably by a 'J39'. The journey was then completed and arrival time at Nottingham Victoria was just after 3.00 am.

The hospital trains

In 1942 the American army built a military hospital on the site of what is now the Kings Mill Hospital in Mansfield. The unit, the first of its type to be built in Britain, was put in a place which was not seen as a high risk enemy target, to deal with troops who had been wounded in conflict. After the Normandy Landings, which commenced in June 1944 with a large number of resulting casualties, the facility was to prove a valuable resource. Wounded were brought to Mansfield by train on the 'Central'. Richard Ford, who was an eyewitness to what happened, comments as follows:

> My grandparents lived in Baums Lane and the house overlooked the railway sidings which were just opposite. Occasionally, in the summer of 1944, as a small boy, I went to stay with them. Sometimes, during the day, a long line of military ambulances would arrive and wait over in the road. Later we would be woken in the night by the noise of a lot of activity. When we looked out from the upstairs bedroom window, we could see that a train had arrived in the sidings. I recall thinking that the carriages seemed to be different from the usual ones and at the end of each one there were blue lights. (Presumably this was because it was the 'blackout' and only a minimum of light was allowed.) As we watched, it was possible to see, in that dim light, soldiers being lifted off the train and transferred to the ambulances which were then driven away.

The Mansfield Railway was clearly helping in the war effort in a very special way.

LNER 'H2' class 4-4-4T No. 6416 stands at the west end of Edwinstowe's island platform with the 7.52 pm train to Nottingham on 8th May, 1946. This locomotive was the last remaining member of the class when withdrawn in November 1947. *H.C. Casserley*

'D2' class 4-4-0 No. 2199 on a local passenger train near Mansfield. The locomotive received the number shown in December 1946 and was withdrawn from service in July 1949. *Jack Cupit*

1945 and the post-war period

After World War II further marked changes in the way people travelled soon became evident. To begin with the railways still had a considerable pre-eminence but this was to be relinquished as the internal combustion engine influenced modes of travel. There were two spheres in which this became particularly significant. The first was in public transport. The increasing and improved number of bus services, notably those being operated by the Trent, East Midland and Mansfield District companies at a local level and also, in addition, improvements in the national bus network as well, inevitably posed a threat. The second, and one which gave rise to a greater threat, related to the rapid growth in the number of family cars. Train services, certainly at local levels, would never be quite the same again and the notion that in the post-war years there would be a return to 'normality' was far from the case for this element of the railways. New norms would emerge and there would be a shift in emphasis.

In 1945 there were eight trains from Nottingham on weekdays. These were: 6.15 and 9.10 am to Edwinstowe; 12.55 pm to Mansfield; 2.15, 4.35 and 5.45 pm to Mansfield; 6.30 pm to Edwinstowe; 9.50 pm to Mansfield. There were seven up trains: trains left Edwinstowe at 7.47, 10.40 am, 1.35 pm and 7.52pm; trains commencing journeys at Mansfield left at 7.14 am, 1.48 pm, and 6.42 pm.

On Sundays there was a service between Nottingham and Mansfield only departing Nottingham at 2.30 and 9.45 pm and departing Mansfield at 11.30 am and 6.37 pm.

In spite of falling passenger numbers, there continued to be a very adequate service provided in the 1950s although with one or two notable exceptions, especially, latterly, during the morning.

The end of an era

Just three years after the war ended, the Government moved to reorganize the railway system in Britain. This was the era when nationalization would be very much the order of the day; state control was considered to be the way forward as the country moved to recover from the ravages of war. The railways were included in this strategy and underwent such nationalization. The LNER, along with the other members of the so-called Great Four, passed into history and became part of British Railways (later to become simply British Rail). By this time, passenger traffic on the Mansfield Railway was certainly declining but definitely not the coal traffic; coal was to become a major factor as economic recovery pressed ahead. Yet it was perhaps inevitable that changes would result, given the changing patterns in society. After World War II with its grim years of austerity, social aspirations together with associated lifestyles would undergo a transition. All these aspects would impinge on Britain's railway system in the following decade and, indeed, thereafter.

Kirkby-in-Ashfield (Central) viewed looking north towards Mansfield in August 1947.
Lens of Sutton Collection

Kirkby-in-Ashfield (Central) viewed looking south towards Nottingham in August 1947.
Lens of Sutton Collection

Chapter Five

Nationalization, 1948 and beyond

When the railways were nationalized in 1948, coal was still reckoned by many to be the king of fuels; in fact it was still often referred to by its long-standing title of 'Old King Coal'; this description had been used in some areas as early as the latter part of the 19th century. The collieries of the East Midlands were some of the most productive and up-to-date in the country and the future looked secure. New collieries were planned and opened to meet the demand for this commodity. One notable case was Bevercotes which involved the extension of a line from Ollerton (part of the Mid-Notts Railway) to serve the mine. Production at the collieries on the Mansfield Railway boomed and the Concentration Sidings near Clipstone were used to capacity. Much of the coal was taken to the power stations which stood along the River Trent, although a great deal of it went considerably further afield. Fish traffic was still an important element. The so called 'fast fish' trains would pass along the line each day. There were, in fact, usually three of these trains, daily. Provision was made for local supplies with one van earmarked for Mansfield, Sutton-in-Ashfield and Kirkby-in-Ashfield. The van was dropped at Mansfield. The story of passenger traffic was, however less encouraging. During the early years of nationalization, numbers using the trains gradually dwindled.

1950 - The accident

Saturday 2nd September, 1950: it was 7.30 am when driver A. Wainwright booked on for duty at Colwick shed (near Nottingham), took charge of class 'N2' No. 69552 and prepared it for the day's duties. He had not had a great deal of experience driving this class of locomotive but what experience he did have led him to believe it was not a difficult class to handle. It was a fine, mild, autumn morning. The prospect for the day ahead promised to be nothing more than routine; straightforward. Everything was in order and quite relaxed. Driver Wainwright was joined by fireman K. Wheatley and No. 69552 was taken off shed and to Nottingham Victoria station on time. At the station, Wainwright backed the engine onto the train and personally coupled the engine to the coaches. There were three coaches, two non-corridor third class brakes and a composite coach between these two. Guard M. Wayman checked the train and all was in order, the brake registering 20 inches of vacuum. Driver Wainwright also tested the brake; 21 inches of vacuum were recorded on the locomotive. The train pulled out of the station on time at 9.18 and there was nothing to suggest anything was amiss, the ride being a smooth one. However, when they got on to the Mansfield branch, Wainwright did think the engine seemed to be oscillating somewhat. Even so, the movement was so slight that he was not particularly concerned. In any case the train was not travelling very fast because the timings were easy. When the train eventually reached

On 2nd September, 1950 the 9.18 am Nottingham (Victoria)-Edwinstowe derailed near Mansfield. 'N2/2' class 0-6-2T No. 69552 plunged down the embankment taking the first two carriages of the train with it. This view shows the scene with two breakdown trains in attendance. The motive power for both breakdown trains is provided by 2-8-0 locomotives, with the larger capacity steam crane in the train nearest to the camera. The line in the background is to Mansfield Colliery.

Transport Treasury

Mansfield station it stood there for two or three minutes. There was a chance to take on water but Wainwright decided this was not necessary; there was enough water in the tank for the journey to Edwinstowe and back.

The train pulled out of Mansfield with just three passengers on board, all of them choosing to sit in the rear coach. As it passed Newgate Lane School, the locomotive was having no difficulty pulling the three coaches up the 1 in 400 gradient and then the 1 in 200 gradient. After a mile the train reached a level section and then went on to a falling gradient of 1 in 160. Wayman commented later that all was normal. The train crew was no doubt relaxed and probably chatting about this and that - the fortunes of 'The Stags' (Mansfield Town Football Club) later that day, perhaps, or the weather or what they would be doing during the coming week. What happened next happened suddenly and came without warning. As the train was approaching Mansfield Colliery (Wainwright had just spotted the down distant signal) the engine lurched to the left and then started to rock violently. Wainwright realized that the engine had derailed. He shouted to Wheatley 'We're off the road'. He then closed the regulator and applied the brake. The section of track on which they were travelling was on an embankment some 10 feet high and both crew realized the engine was about to plunge down it. In what must have seemed like an eternity, Wainwright clung on to the cab and Wheatley hung on to the brake handle. The locomotive overturned but, incredibly, both men survived the fall. Meanwhile, guard Wayman had been looking out of the window enjoying the view when the last coach gave a jerk and began to roll from side to side. He jumped up to apply the brake but it was already on. The two leading coaches both followed the engine off the track and down the embankment. Mercifully, the third coach, in which all the passengers were travelling, remained on the track, tilting at 20 degrees. Eighty yards of track had been destroyed, a further 30 had been distorted and a small underbridge was damaged. It seems assistance was quick in arriving. The passengers, unhurt but no doubt badly shaken, were soon on the way to their destinations, single line working was in place by 11.15 am, the rear coach was re-railed, the down track repaired and normal working was operational by 7.20 pm that day. The engine and two coaches remained where they were until Sunday 10th September.

The scene of the accident caused quite a stir, locally, and many people paid a visit. The author recalls being taken, as a small boy, to view the result of the crash. The sight of the huge - or so it seemed - locomotive, not dissimilar to the Hornby-Dublo tank engine he was familiar with, lying helplessly on its side at the bottom of the embankment made a lasting impression. But what had been the cause? Why had the engine suddenly so unexpectedly behaved in this way?

Brigadier C.A. Langley carried out the investigation for the Ministry of Transport. The accident report was issued in 1951. The brigadier looked at likely causes and several seemed to be possible. Regarding the locomotive:

> There was considerable superficial damage to the engine; the bunker and cab were dented, the brake and other undergear were twisted and the right-hand leading and driving wheels were badly scored where they had struck the left-hand rail of the track but the most significant damage occurred on the left-hand trailing coupled wheel and the axle box tee link was bent backwards the keep pin was bent and the brass axle box was fractured on its leading side...

Brigadier Langley goes on to say that one possibility was that some object had been responsible for this damage. However, it was by no means clear whether the damage had occurred before or during or after the derailment. He goes on to say later: 'The 'N2' class, which has been in service for some 30 years, has been known as a type liable to hunt' and he quotes instances where this appears to have caused derailments. The phenomenon described as 'hunting' occurs when a wheel flange hits the rail and rebounds, resulting in the wheel at the opposite end of the axle doing the same. This means that in addition to forward motion there is a side to side oscillation. Hunting is usually associated with high speeds.

Nevertheless, the brigadier points out that it is not a commonly experienced phenomenon because these engines were mainly employed in places such as King's Cross where the track was maintained to a high standard and the engines travelled chimney-first up the gradient and bunker first on the downward and faster journey. After considering the evidence, Brigadier Langley concludes:

> There is no evidence ... to suggest that the train was traveling at high speed ... I am satisfied that the train was being driven under proper control and at a reasonable speed ... Examination of the engine after the accident showed that the frame was true, the tyres were in good condition and there had been little wear on the coupled wheels. The pony truck sideplay was however excessive with a total movement of 11/16 inches before the helical restraining springs could come into play ...this would allow the trailing end of the engine to swing much more than normal [other critical details are then listed].
>
> Although the past history of this type of engine shows that it has a tendency to hunt, I doubt whether the above defects alone were in themselves sufficient to have caused derailment at modest speed.
>
> The track generally was in good condition for a class 'C' line. The rails had worn evenly, the sleepers were sound, the fastenings were holding well and there was no sign of chair movement or gauge spreading except on the distorted section.
>
> There were a number of low points on the curve but the only material defect was a variation in the cross level which was remarkably regular. The actual difference in level at any one point was not excessive, the maximum being 5/8 inch. The effect however was to produce sudden variations in cant gradient on the level track varying from 1 inch in 40 feet to 1 inch in 25 feet.
>
> The latter is high for a speed of 60 mph, the maximum for the branch but would not have been excessive at 40 mph the maximum probable speed of the train. The cross level variations would undoubtedly cause some lurching but this should not have become dangerous on a properly balanced engine, when running at a comparatively low speed.
>
> The distortion of the track immediately before the point of derailment could not have been caused by heat stresses because the temperature on the day of the accident was moderate.
>
> The unusual damage to the left trailing coupled wheel and spring buckle might lead one to think that the accident was due to an obstruction. The jamming of an L-shaped object such as a half chair between the wheel and the spring would have momentarily locked this pair of wheels which in turn would have skidded the other coupled wheels and probably twisted the engine slightly. These reactions coupled with the violent disturbance of weights when the axle box broke might well have caused the derailment. And the heavy lurch felt by both enginemen would have been consistent with this theory [however] if this had been the case I would not have expected the track to have

been distorted and it is even more difficult to conceive how a heavy object such as a chair or substantial piece of metal could have been thrown up from the track. The previous express had passed safely over the line.

The train referred to here was the 8.25 from Leicester to Scarborough. It was made up of a class 'B1' locomotive hauling 12 coaches. Later examination of that train did not show anything of an unusual nature. The brigadier then considered combined locomotive and track defects and concluded:

> Derailments on straight track at moderate speeds are most unusual unless due to serious locomotive or track defects. Neither of these factors was present in this case and ... I do not think that an obstruction can be accepted as a simple solution of the problem. The cause must therefore be sought in an analysis of the effects of track conditions on an engine which had probably become particularly sensitive to them.

He then makes an observation which may have prompted driver Wheatley to regret not having topped up the water tanks at Mansfield although he was in no way to blame for not having done so,

> It is likely that the low joints on the curve set up some minor oscillations which might have been increased slightly by surging of water in the half-full tanks. These initial movements would not have become serious until the engine passed from the curve on to the straight, where regular change in the cross levels would have increased the oscillations. This build up must have been unusually rapid and was probably due to the short pitch of the cant variations over the last 140 feet synchronizing with the periodicity of the engine at a comparatively low speed.

He then comments and concludes,

> Finally the past history of this class of engine leads one to think it is of a type which reacts unfavorably to uneven track ... It is therefore reasonable to conclude that by rare mischance all the unfavorable factors were working together on this occasion so as to produce dangerous conditions at a normally safe speed.

So nobody was to blame - except the locomotive! In his recommendations, Brigadier Langley stated,

> It must not be thought that because of this accident the running of 'N2' engines on secondary lines is dangerous. As already explained, the conditions in this case were most unusual ... This derailment, however, emphasizes, once again, that in certain circumstances the 'N2' engine is unduly sensitive to track irregularities such as may be found on secondary lines.

He went on to recommend that if the class was used on these branches, consideration should be given to more frequent examination of springs and bearings so that side play did not become excessive and that the speed at which these locomotives were operated on secondary lines should be limited. He also expressed the view that as far as the Mansfield branch was concerned, unless the track could be fettled more frequently than every six months, as appeared to be the practice, the maximum speed should be reduced from 60 mph.

On 23rd July, 1953, 'N7/5' class 0-6-2T No. 69654 hauls a local passenger train away from Kirkby South Junction on the Mansfield Railway and towards Kirkby-in-Ashfield Central. Although there has been considerable vegetation growth on this site, it is still recognisable. *Frank Ashley*

During the mid-1950s, 'N1' class 0-6-2T No. 69481 enters Kirkby-in-Ashfield Central with a local passenger train for Nottingham Victoria. *Jack Cupit*

1952

In 1952 there were seven weekday trains out of Nottingham using all or some of the route. In summary these were:

Ex-Nottingham	To	Arrive
6.15 am	Edwinstowe	7.24 am (with a Lincoln connection)
9.18 am	Edwinstowe	10.18 am (Saturdays only)
1.15 pm	Mansfield	1.55 pm
2.38 pm	Edwinstowe	3.39 pm
4.35 pm	Mansfield	5.18 pm
5.45 pm	Mansfield	6.36 pm
6.54 pm	Edwinstowe	7.56 pm
10.07 pm	Mansfield	10.43 pm

Some of the timings on Saturdays varied from the weekday ones by a few minutes. In this period there were eight up trains on weekdays (there was no Sunday service):

Ex	Departing	Arriving Nottingham	
Mansfield	7.15 am	7.53 am	
Edwinstowe	7.55 am	8.56 am	
Edwinstowe	10.40 am	11.39 am	Saturdays only
Mansfield	1.18 pm	2.02 pm	
Mansfield	2.24 pm	3.05 pm	
Ollerton	3.22 pm	4.35 pm	
Edwinstowe	4.45 pm	5.46 pm	
Mansfield	6.50 pm	7.33 pm	
Edwinstowe	8.07 pm	9.09 pm	
Mansfield	11.50 pm	12.27 am	Fridays only*

* The purpose of this train was to give a connection with the overnight summer season train from Nottingham to Ramsgate.

However, by this time there were good regular bus services being operated. The Trent Bus Co. covered the area to the west and south of Mansfield with a regular service between Mansfield and Nottingham. The East Midland company, Ebor, Bakers and Wass Bros covered the area further east, linking Mansfield with Clipstone, Ollerton and Retford. The Midland General also linked Mansfield to Nottingham via a more tortuous route than the Trent company but taking in Basford, with the overall result that a large number of towns and villages were linked to Nottingham by convenient bus services. Kirkby-in-Ashfield was served by the Midland General and Trent companies, Mansfield District Traction took care of the Mansfield connection with Sutton-in-Ashfield. These services were inevitably going to make inroads into the railway operation but there soon emerged another very significant factor which would also eventually seriously reduce even the bus operators' hold on the market. This other factor was the private motor car. Cars became more readily available to larger numbers of people in this period and in an era when petrol

'N5' class 0-6-2T No. 69311 shunting at Clipstone Sidings in the early 1950s. This was one of the few members of the class which had extended tanks and larger bunkers and cabs. It was withdrawn in February 1952.
Jack Cupit

'J6' class 0-6-0 No. 64212 on an engineer's train. Reballasting work is taking place at the junction of the Mansfield Railway and the GCR main line at Kirkby South on a Sunday afternoon in the 1950s.
Frank Ashley

'O4/8' class 2-8-0 No. 63877 approaches Clipstone East Junction signal box with a coal train on 7th November, 1964.
H.B. Priestley/W. Taylor

'O2/2' class 2-8-0 No. 63945 with a Frodingham to Newport, south Wales steel train leaving the Mansfield Railway at Kirkby South Junction and joining the GCR line to pass through Annesley tunnel.
Frank Ashley

'B1' class 4-6-0 No. 61125 hauls a Hull to Plymouth fish train and is passing over the Pinxton branch en route for Kirkby South Junction. *Phil Robinson/John Hitchens Collection*

'Britannia' class 4-6-2 No. 70035 *Rudyard Kipling* leaves Mansfield, southbound, with a fish train in the late 1950s. *Jack Cupit*

was very cheap. All these factors had a devastating impact on the line still usually referred to as the 'Central', as they did all over the country. By 1955 it had been decided the passenger services on the Mansfield Railway were no longer viable. It was reckoned that even without the factors mentioned already, there was another element, namely a perfectly adequate train service on the Midland line, at least as far as the Mansfield - Nottingham service was concerned. Mansfield, by now a thriving and growing town, would not be left without a rail connection. It was simply a matter of rationalizing from two down to one.

The 'Fast Fish' trains

Further mention must be made of the so called 'fast fish' trains, referred to earlier, which used the line. In the latter years they became something of a legend. These trains, carrying their very perishable commodity, would race down from Grimsby and Hull, clatter onto the line at Clipstone, scurry past Clipstone and Crown Farm (Mansfield) collieries and on through Mansfield (dropping off a van) storm on to Sutton and Kirkby and there would leave the line and dash on to their destinations. Towards the end of their time, Gresley 'K3' 2-6-0 and 'B1' 4-6-0 classes hauled them. In the late 1950s the afternoon 'Fast Fish' was considered to be something rather special by schoolboys (including the author) in Mansfield, who used to rush from school to see it pass. The 'myth', for such it seems to have been, was that this was a possible opportunity (probably the only one at that time) to see a named engine on this line at Mansfield.

R. Beeton writes,

> Every evening at 20.50 (we called it ten to nine in those days) the 'Banbury fish' would rattle past behind a Grimsby 'K3', drop a wagon at Mansfield station and tear off to Woodford Halse where it would change loco and crew for a Great Western combination. You could and did set your watch by this fast perishable goods, winter or summer; it was always on time, running to a fast passenger schedule.

The comment here about the timing is borne out by others. One made the observation that when the 'fast fish' went by you looked at your watch; not to check whether the fish was on time or not but rather whether your watch was right.

There have been suggestions that it was the 'fast fish' trains, able to carry this easily perishable commodity still fresh to a diversity of destinations, that did much for the promotion of the 'fish and chip' culture that has been an epitome of the British way of life. There may be some truth in this but the procedure of encasing fish in a batter had been around long before the railways appeared although it is not really possible to say with certainty (in spite of a number of claims) when the chips were added! However, there may have been some boost when, during World War II, Winston Churchill decreed that fish and chips must be still available because that staple diet of the British people would help to maintain morale.

'Britannia' class 4-6-2 No. 70039 *Sir Christopher Wren* at Kirkby South Junction on 1st May, 1963 with an Immingham-Whitland fish train.
Roger Jones

Bill Brownhill who was the booking clerk at Kirkby-in-Ashfield Central and was responsible for the prize-winning station gardens in the early 1950s. He had lost part of an arm in an accident but this did not deter him.
Fred Maltby

1955

In this, the last year in which passenger services were operated there was, again, little change, although none of the trains ran through to Ollerton.

Down service

Nottingham dep.	Destination		Arrive
6.08 am	Edwinstowe		7.17 am
9.18 am	Edwinstowe	Saturday only	10.18 am
10.07 am	Mansfield	Except Wednesday and Saturday	10.43 am
10.45 am	Mansfield	Wednesday and Saturday only	11.21 am
12.25 pm	Mansfield		1.03 pm
1.15 pm	Mansfield		1.55 pm
2.38 pm	Edwinstowe		3.39 pm
4.14 pm	Mansfield	Saturday only	4.50 pm
4.35 pm	Mansfield	Except Saturday	5.18 pm
5.44 pm	Mansfield		6.26 pm
6.54 pm	Mansfield		7.36 pm

Up service

Ex	Depart		Arrive
Mansfield	7.14 am	Ran through to Leicester	8.51 am
Edwinstowe	8.00 am		9.01 am
Edwinstowe	10.40 am	Saturdays only	11.39 am
Mansfield	1.18 pm		2.02 pm
Mansfield	2.24 pm		3.05 pm
Edwinstowe	4.33 pm	Except Saturday	5.41 pm
Edwinstowe	4.48 pm	Saturday only	5.49 pm
Mansfield	6.50 pm		7.33 pm
Mansfield	8.25 pm		9.09 pm

All, apart from the 7.14 am, terminated at Nottingham. There were no Sunday trains.

In October, an interim timetable was produced and times varied slightly from those for the period from June to September. The interim timetable did not give a service east of Mansfield but there is evidence that, in practice, some trains continued to run through to Edwinstowe until passenger services ceased at the end of December. In addition to these 'locals', there was a batch of summer holiday trains to a variety of destinations.

The end of scheduled passenger services

The last passenger train ran on New Year's Eve 1955. Motive power on this occasion was provided by class 'L1' No. 67799 but although there had been some opposition by local traders to the proposed closure and there was some activity to mark the event there seems, in general, to have been little reaction. Nobody, for example, saw fit to place a wreath on the engine, a practice which was to become all too commonplace on similar occasions in later years. Bill Brownhill (at Kirkby-in-Ashfield) put up a notice to the effect that 'The oldest thing on display is the booking clerk - who has no objection to being preserved' (*see page 120*). Souvenir tickets were on sale and the local press waxed eloquent.

'J6' class 0-6-0 No. 64202 departing Mansfield with a Nottingham (Victoria) to Edwinstowe passenger train on 30th April, 1955. *John Cupit*

'N1' class 0-6-2T No. 69469 at Sutton-in-Ashfield (Central) with the 2.24 pm from Mansfield on 14th May, 1955. *H.B. Priestley/ courtesy W. Taylor*

'B1' class 4-6-0 No. 61063 waits to leave Mansfield (Central) with a train for Nottingham (Victoria). *T.G. Hepburn/Rail Archive Stephenson*

'B1' class 4-6-0 No. 61066 waits to leave Mansfield (Central) with a train for Nottingham (Victoria). *T.G. Hepburn/Rail Archive Stephenson*

A 'J6' 0-6-0 runs round its train at Mansfield (Central) after arrival from Nottingham (Victoria) on 12th December, 1955.
John P. Wilson/Rail Archive Stephenson

A 'J6' 0-6-0 at Mansfield (Central) with a train from Nottingham (Victoria) on 12th December, 1955.
John P. Wilson/Rail Archive Stephenson

'K3' class 2-6-0 No. 61975 passes Clipstone East Junction with a Nottingham (Victoria) to Edwinstowe train on 17th September, 1955. *T.G. Hepburn/Rail Archive Stephenson*

'A5' class 4-6-2T No. 69810 waits to leave Mansfield (Central) with the 2.24 pm train for Nottingham (Victoria) on 3rd December, 1955. *T.G.Hepburn/Rail Archive Stephenson*

Kirkby-in-Ashfield (Central) station on 31st December, 1955.

John P. Wilson/Rail Archive Stephenson

'A5' class 4-6-2T No. 69807 at Sutton-in-Ashfield (Central) with the 1.26 pm train to Nottingham (Victoria) on 31st December, 1955.   *T.G.Hepburn/Rail Archive Stephenson*

'Was it a tear which fell from the whistle of engine 67799 or merely steam condensing after the last mournful sound had pierced the gloomy corners of the near deserted Central station?', wrote one reporter. The driver, Cyril Peet and fireman, Eddie Grocock, together with guard R. Cox were the crew and 'a handful' of people took the opportunity to join the train as it returned to New Basford with what would normally have been empty stock. 'Dead on time as the bells of Saint Wilfrid's parish church at Kirkby-in-Ashfield were ringing the Old Year out and the New Year in, the regular passenger train on the Mansfield-Nottingham Central line left the Kirkby-in-Ashfield Central station after calling at Sutton-in-Ashfield on its last run to Nottingham'. It was often the case that at the time of closure, an enthusiasts' special was run and this also happened on the Mansfield Railway. This special, organized by the LCGB, was hauled by two class 'B1' engines (Nos. 61139 and 61177) and was the last passenger train to use the up line of the Mansfield Railway. Following the closure, which it was reckoned would save £28,000, the residents of Sutton-in-Ashfield petitioned successfully for the reopening of Sutton Town station (ex-GNR) for general passenger traffic. (It was still providing a valuable week-end service for Saturday-only football and shoppers excursions.) Facilities for goods traffic were withdrawn from Kirkby-in-Ashfield and Sutton-in-Ashfield Central at the same time although the Helical Bar Co. took over the former and used the station building on the up side as office accommodation. This company used the rail link and the siding at Sutton. In the meantime British Railways converted the ladies waiting room on the down side into a booking office for the holiday and excursion trains. This was manned by a clerk from Sutton Junction with a porter from Sutton Town station.

The empty stock of the last passenger train waits to depart from Mansfield station on 31st December, 1955. It was hauled by 'L1' class 2-6-4T No. 67799.   *Frank Ashley*

SPECIAL NOTICE

BRITISH RAILWAYS, London Midland Region regret that after careful consideration it has been decided that on and from

Monday, 2nd January, 1956

THE ORDINARY PASSENGER TRAIN SERVICE BETWEEN

Nottingham Victoria and Edwinstowe

WILL BE WITHDRAWN

and the following stations will be closed for all Passenger Traffic except Special Excursion and Summer Holiday trains:—

MANSFIELD CENTRAL
SUTTON-IN-ASHFIELD CENTRAL
KIRKBY-IN-ASHFIELD CENTRAL
EDWINSTOWE

Alternative facilities for Passengers will be available from Mansfield Town, Sutton Junction, Kirkby Bentinck or Kirkby-in-Ashfield East stations or by local omnibus services operated by:—

EAST MIDLANDS MOTOR SERVICES LTD.
MANSFIELD DISTRICT TRACTION CO.
MIDLAND GENERAL OMNIBUS CO., LTD.
TRENT MOTOR TRACTION CO., LTD.

On and from the same date the following Goods Depots will ALSO BE CLOSED:—
SUTTON-IN-ASHFIELD CENTRAL
KIRKBY-IN-ASHFIELD CENTRAL

Alternative arrangements have been made for dealing with Parcels and Freight Train traffic, details of which will be displayed at each of the stations concerned.

BRITISH RAILWAYS

LADIES & GENTLEMEN WITH FURTHER REFERENCE TO THE CLOSING DOWN OF THE RLY SERVICE ON THE MANSFIELD LINE WE WOULD LIKE TO SAY THAT THE NEAREST APPROACH TO WHAT YOU REQUIRE AS A SOUVENIR IS A L.N.E.R SINGLE TICKET TO MANSFIELD WHICH WOULD COST YOU 10^d

THE MOST ANCIENT THING AS A MOMENTO WE COULD OFFER WOULD OF COURSE BE THE CLERK & HE GIVES US TO UNDERSTAND HE WOULD HAVE NO OBJECTIONS TO BEING REGARDED AS A CURIOSITY OR BEING PRESERVED

Bill Brownhill's chalkboard notice at Kirkby-in-Ashfield.

Excursions trains after World War II

After the war ended in 1945, the special holiday and excursion trains were re-introduced during the summer months and these were still run for a time after regular passenger services ceased. In the summer of 1957, for example, there were Saturday holiday trains to Bridlington, Cleethorpes, Filey, Mablethorpe, Scarborough, Skegness and Yarmouth. The Skegness train left Bulwell Common at 6.47 am calling at Mansfield at 7.22, Edwinstowe at 7.42 and Ollerton at 7.48 am. It reached its destination at 9.48 am. The train for Mablethorpe arrived there at 10.18 am, having left Bulwell Common at 7.01 am and calling at Mansfield at 7.35 am. The one for Cleethorpes left Leicester at 7.20, called at Nottingham at 8.00 am, Mansfield at 8.45 am and arrived at Cleethorpes at 11.09 am. The Bridlington, Filey and Scarborough train also started at Leicester. It left at 7.45 am and reached Mansfield at 9.13 am. Arrival at Bridlington was at 12.33 pm, Filey at 1.02 and Scarborough at 1.23 pm. There was also a later train to Bridlington and Scarborough which left Bulwell Common at 9.23 am and Mansfield at 9.54. Return trains left Mablethorpe at 11.50 am (going to Basford North), Cleethorpes (for Leicester) at 1.23 pm, Skegness (for Bulwell) at 2.12 pm, Scarborough (for Basford North and calling at Filey and Bridlington) at 2.35 pm. There was also a connecting service to Nottingham Victoria for a Ramsgate train which ran over-night on Fridays in the summer. Passengers from Mansfield, Sutton and Kirkby had a connecting service which left Mansfield at 11.50 pm. They changed at Nottingham Victoria onto a train which had started in Derby and left Nottingham at 12.45 am. There were calls at Loughborough, Leicester, Lutterworth, Rugby (Central) and Woodford Halse and the (probably weary) holiday-makers alighted at Herne Bay with Whitstable and Tankerton, Birchington-on-Sea, Westgate-on-Sea, Margate, Broadstairs, Dumpton Park and Ramsgate (where they arrived at 6.56 am). The return journey was less onerous with departure from Ramsgate at 12.10 pm and a through journey to Mansfield, arriving at 7.40 pm. Before 1950 there had been a similar train which ran overnight from Mansfield through to Clacton-on-Sea.

These holiday trains were withdrawn from the Mansfield Railway line after the summer of 1962 and in 1963 were transferred to the Midland and joined the former LD&ECR at Shirebrook.

In addition to the holiday trains, many day excursions were run. These were often to seaside destinations on the east coast including not only the obvious ones such as Skegness but also places such as Filey. On Whit Mondays there were excursions bringing visitors in from Nottingham Victoria to Ollerton and Edwinstowe and half-day excursions to Sherwood Forest. As well as the day trips to the east coast there were ones to the Schoolboys Internationals at Wembley; all advertised on special leaflets. Ian Allan organized visits for train-spotters to places such as the Doncaster railway works and large numbers would travel from Mansfield and district on these special trains. There is an account of what was described as a 'Photographers' Excursion' which, on one occasion, ran from Burton-on-Trent along the Mansfield Railway and eventually ended up at Windermere, having taken the western curve at Clipstone and travelled by way of Sheffield Victoria, the Woodhead tunnel,

A 'B1' class 4-6-0 hauls a northbound Ian Allan excursion to Doncaster works into Kirkby-in-Ashfield (Central) on 9th April, 1953. *John Hitchens*

'B1' class 4-6-0 No. 61283 at Kirkby-in-Ashfield (Central) station, with the Attenborough Model Railway Club Locospotters Excursion to Swindon works in 1953. *John Hitchens*

The preserved GNR 'C1' class 4-4-2 No. 251, pilots a former GCR 'Director' 'D11' class 4-4-0 No. 62663 *Prince Albert* on a Northern Rubber Co. 'Farnborough Flyer' on 12th September, 1954. The 'Director' is taking on water at Mansfield (Central) station. *Jack Cupit*

The Royal Observer Corps' 'Farnborough Flyer' organized by Alan Pegler (the first person to privately-own *Flying Scotsman*) departs from Mansfield (Central) on 11th September, 1955. Two 'D11' class 4-4-0s haul the train, the pilot engine being No. 62666 *Zeebrugge* and 62667 *Somme* is the train engine. *Jack Cupit*

A330/R(H.D.)

PLEASE RETAIN THIS BILL FOR REFERENCE.

CHEAP TRIPS
TO
EDWINSTOWE
AND
OLLERTON
(For the DUKERIES)

WHIT SUNDAY & MONDAY
29th & 30th MAY 1955

FROM	TIMES OF DEPARTURE		RETURN FARES Third Class to		ARRIVAL TIMES ON RETURN	
	29th May	30th May	Edwinstowe	Ollerton	29th May	30th May
	pm	pm	s d	s d		
PINXTON South	...	1A12	4/6	4/6		9A14
PYE HILL & SOMERCOTES	...	1A17	4/3	4/3		9A11
JACKSDALE	...	1A20	4/3	4/3		9A 8
EASTWOOD & LANGLEY MILL	...	1A30	4/-	4/-		9A 1
NEWTHORPE	...	1A33	3/9	3/9		8A57
KIMBERLEY East	...	1A40	3/3	3/3		8A52
BASFORD North	...	1A48	3/3	3/3		8A45
NOTTINGHAM Victoria	12 50	2 15	3/-	3/-	8 2	8 5
BULWELL Central	12 58	2 24	2/9	2/9	7 54	7 57
HUCKNALL Central	1 4	2 31	2/9	2/9	7 48	7 50
KIRKBY-IN-ASHFIELD Central	1 16	2 44	2/-	2/3	7 36	7 38
SUTTON-IN-ASHFIELD	1 21	2 49	1/9	2/-	7 30	7 31
MANSFIELD Central	1 28	2 56	1/6	1/9	7 22	7 20
			Passengers return same day at			
EDWINSTOWE arrive	1 46	3 14			pm	pm
OLLERTON	1 50	3 17			7 0	7 0

A—Passengers change at NOTTINGHAM Victoria in each direction. On the outward journey going forward at 2.15 pm and on return at 8.37 pm.

CHILDREN under three years of age, free; three years and under fourteen, half-fare.

NOTICE AS TO CONDITIONS
These tickets are issued subject to the British Transport Commission's published Regulations and Conditions applicable to British Railways, exhibited at their stations or obtainable free of charge at Station Booking Offices.

For LUGGAGE ALLOWANCES see these Regulations and Conditions.

RAIL TICKETS CAN BE OBTAINED IN ADVANCE AT STATIONS AND AGENCIES

Further information will be supplied on application to Stations, Agencies, or to W. B. CARTER, District Commercial Manager, DERBY. Telephone: Derby 42442, Extn. 204; or NOTTINGHAM Victoria. Telephone: Nottingham 44381, Extn. 52.

Travel in Rail Comfort

BRITISH RAILWAYS

April 1955

Arthur Gaunt & Sons (Printers) Ltd., Heanor, Derbyshire.

BR 35000

A576/R(H.D.)

PLEASE RETAIN THIS BILL FOR REFERENCE.

CHEAP TRIP
TO
YORK
AND
SCARBOROUGH

SUNDAY 31st JULY 1955

FROM	TIMES OF DEPARTURE	RETURN FARES Third Class to		ARRIVAL TIMES ON RETURN	
		York	Scarborough	York	Scarborough
	am	s d	s d	pm	pm
NOTTINGHAM Victoria	9 28	10/6	16/3	10 35	10 35
NEW BASFORD	9 34	10/6	16/3	10 28	10 28
BULWELL COMMON	9 40	10/6	15/6	10 22	10 22
HUCKNALL Central	9 47	9/6	15/3	10 15	10 15
KIRKBY-IN-ASHFIELD Central	10 0				
SUTTON-IN-ASHFIELD Central	10 7	9/-	14/6	10 2	10 2
MANSFIELD Central	10 14	9/-	14/6	9 55	9 55
	pm				
YORK arrive	12 28	Passengers return same day at		7 46	7 46
SCARBOROUGH Londesborough Road	1 30	" " " "		6 48	6 48

CHILDREN under three years of age, free; three years and under fourteen, half-fare.

NOTICE AS TO CONDITIONS
These tickets are issued subject to the British Transport Commission's published Regulations and Conditions applicable to British Railways, exhibited at their stations or obtainable free of charge at Station Booking Offices.

For LUGGAGE ALLOWANCES see these Regulations and Conditions.

RAIL TICKETS CAN BE OBTAINED IN ADVANCE AT STATIONS AND AGENCIES

Further information will be supplied on application to Stations, Agencies, Official Railway Agents, or to W. B. CARTER, District Commercial Manager, DERBY. Telephone: Derby 42442, Extn. 204; or NOTTINGHAM Victoria, Telephone: Nottingham 44381, Extn. 52.

Travel in Rail Comfort

BRITISH RAILWAYS

July 1955

Arthur Gaunt & Sons (Printers) Ltd., Heanor, Derbyshire.

BR 35000

NATIONALIZATION, 1948 AND BEYOND

In the 1950s 'B1' class 4-6-0 No. 61088 is seen with a returning seaside excursion, having just left the Kirkby-in-Ashfield (Central) station which is round the corner on the right of the photograph. The whole area has now been landscaped. *Frank Ashley*

A holiday special arrives at Sutton-in-Ashfield behind 'K1' class 2-6-0 No. 62040 in the early 1950s. *T.G. Hepburn/Rail Archive Stephenson*

'K3' 2-6-0 No. 61844 calls at Sutton-in-Ashfield (Central) with a Skegness excursion in the early 1950s. *T.G. Hepburn/Rail Archive Stephenson*

'K1' class 2-6-0 No 62040 at Sutton-in-Ashfield (Central) with a Skegness excursion in the early 1950s. *T.G. Hepburn/Rail Archive Stephenson*

skirted Manchester and then joined the West Coast main line. It was not without significance that the Central line was chosen for the Sunday excursions from Mansfield and district to the east coast, rather than the Midland. Using the Midland line would have required the opening of at least eight signal boxes whereas the Central line (which, for example, had no level crossings) needed only the Mansfield box before the line reached Clipstone junction, so effecting an economy.

Excursions were still being run during the 1960s for Clipstone Colliery employees and their children. In August these ran from Clipstone Colliery sidings to Cleethorpes and Skegness and usually involved up to three trains. R. Beeton recalls,

> I well remember going on summertime excursions to the Lincolnshire coast, usually behind a Doncaster K3 from Mansfield Central via Lincoln at a cost of 4s. 6d. per adult – full day; 2s. 6d. – half day (after mid-day) and 1s. 6d. - evening (after 4 pm). All returning departures between 11.30 pm and midnight.

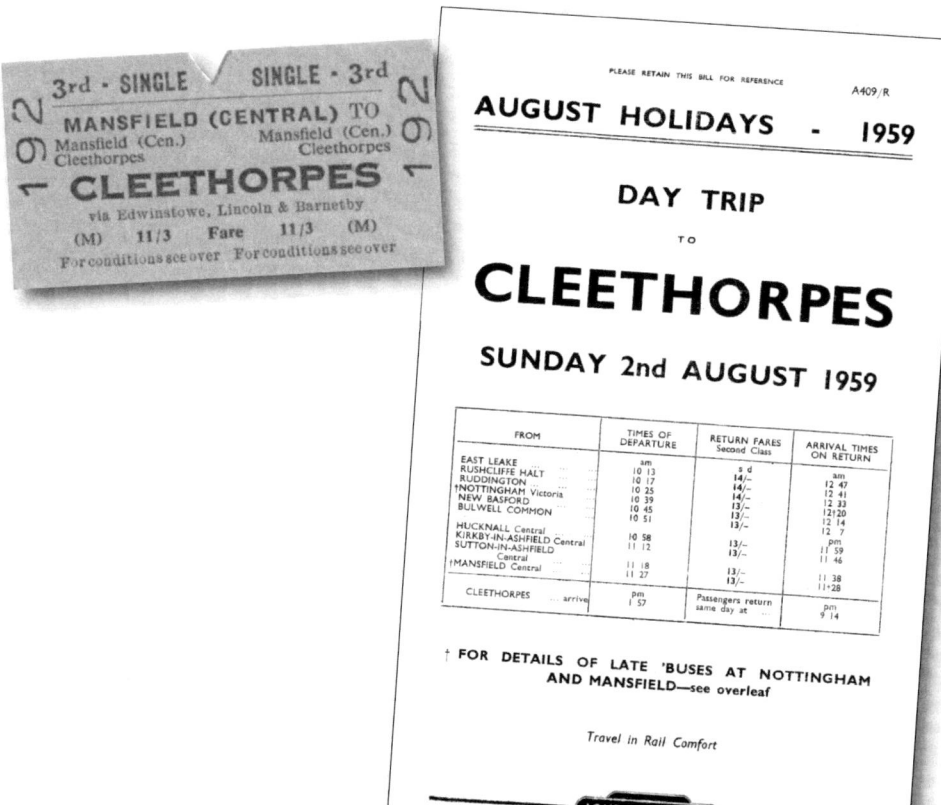

'K3/2' 2-6-0 No. 61990 is near Sherwood Hall with a Kirkby-Skegness excursion on 27th May, 1958. *Jack Cupit*

Double-headed Thompson 'B1' class 4-6-0s Nos. 61173 and 61131 on the 'Great Central Railtour' run down to Kirkby South Junction on the last day of Great Central main line steam, 3rd September, 1966. This train originated at London (Waterloo) and was hauled to Nottingham (Victoria) behind the Southern Region's 'Merchant Navy' class 4-6-2 No. 35030 *Elder Dempster Lines*. From there to Elsecar Junction (via Staveley) Nos. 61173 and 61131 took charge. Electric locomotive 'EM1' class B-B No E26021 continued to Penistone and then headed to Sheffield (Victoria). At Sheffield the 'B1s' were reunited with the train and returned to Nottingham via Woodhouse East Junction, Killamarsh Junction, Clowne South, Langwith Junction, Clipstone West Junction, Mansfield and Kirkby South Junction. *Elder Dempster Lines* then returned the train to London, terminating at Marylebone station. *John Hitchens*

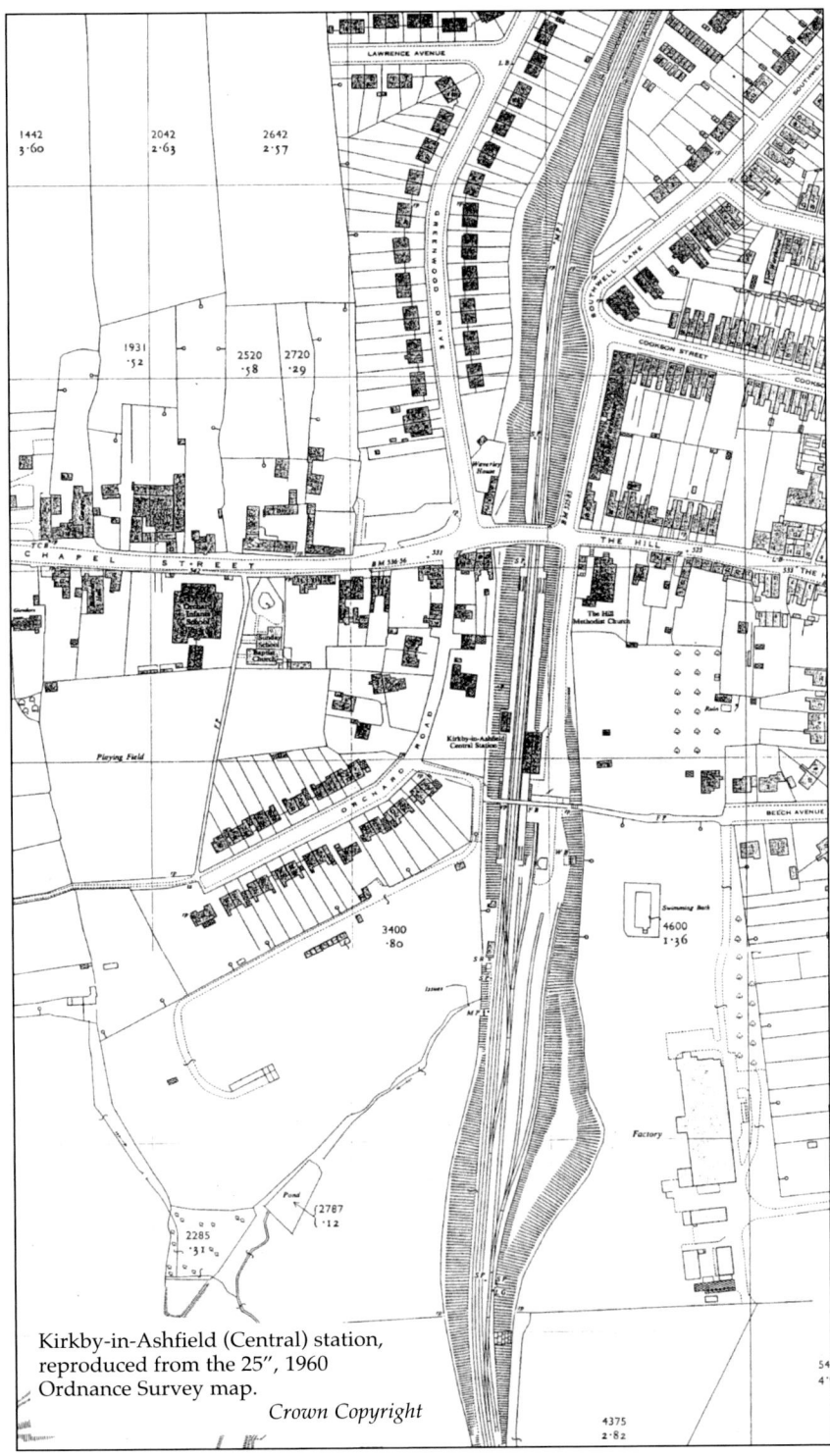

Kirkby-in-Ashfield (Central) station, reproduced from the 25", 1960 Ordnance Survey map. *Crown Copyright*

Sutton-in Ashfield (Central) signal box. *Author's Collection*

Looking south at Sutton-in-Ashfield (Central) station on 4th May, 1957. Empty wagons have been stored on both lines. The area is now buried below the A38 road.
Phil Robinson/John Hitchens Collection

NATIONALIZATION, 1948 AND BEYOND

Kirkby-in-Ashfield station after closure to passengers with a rake of hopper wagons.
Author's Collection

Mansfield (Central) station in the mid-1960s. *Maurice Billington/Industrial Railway Society*

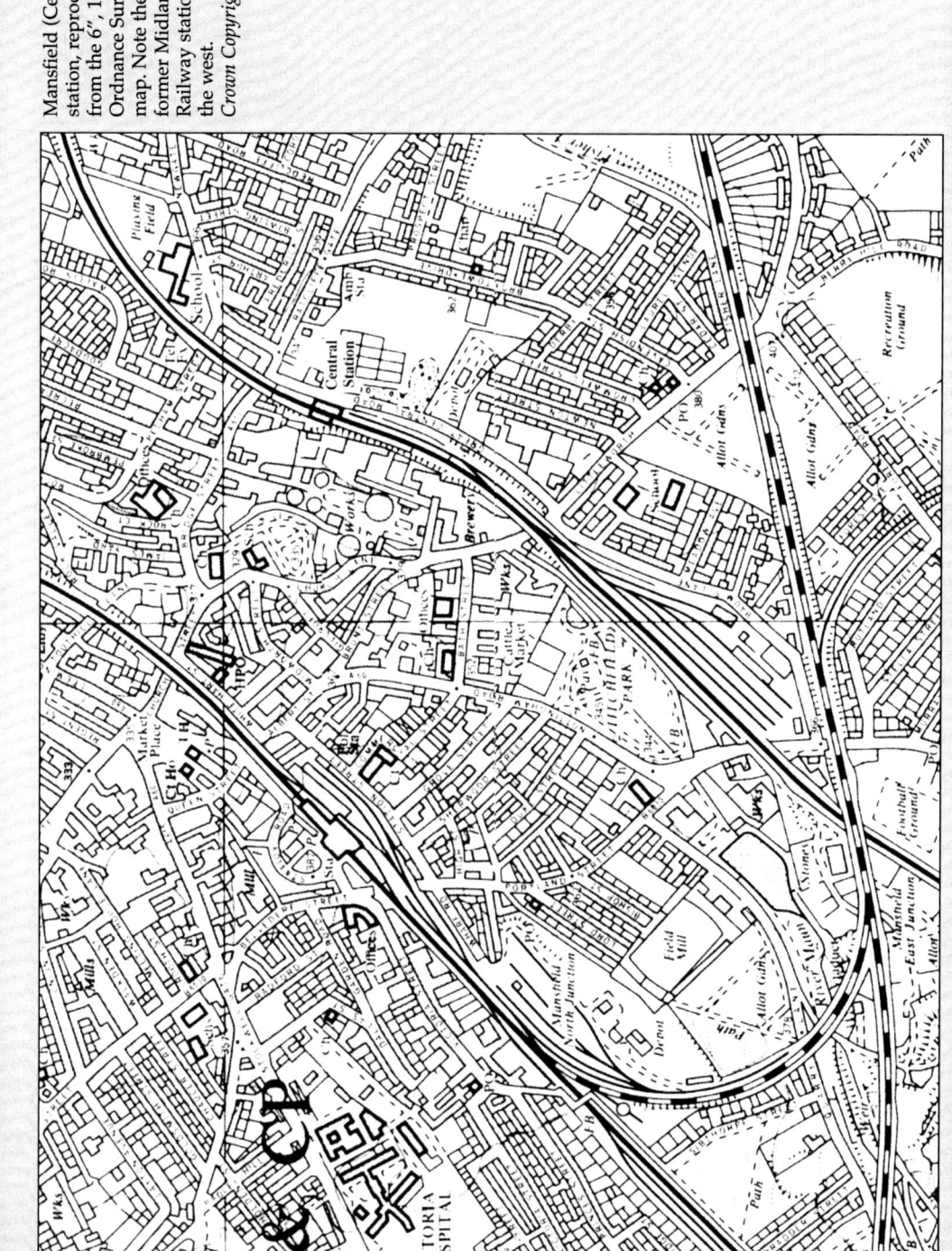

Mansfield (Central) station, reproduced from the 6", 1967 Ordnance Survey map. Note the former Midland Railway station to the west. *Crown Copyright*

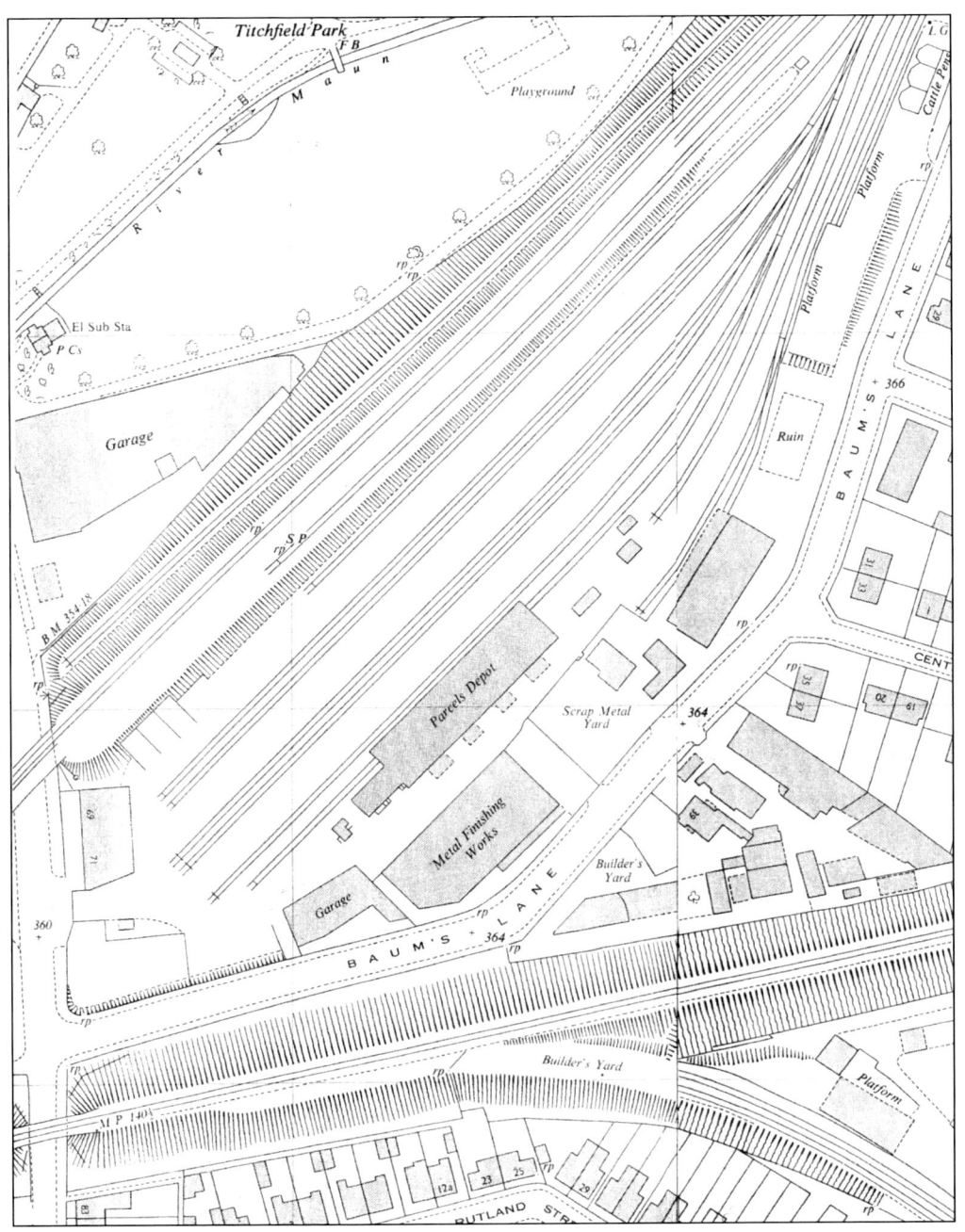

Mansfield (Central) goods yard, reproduced from the 25" Ordnance Survey map.
Crown Copyright

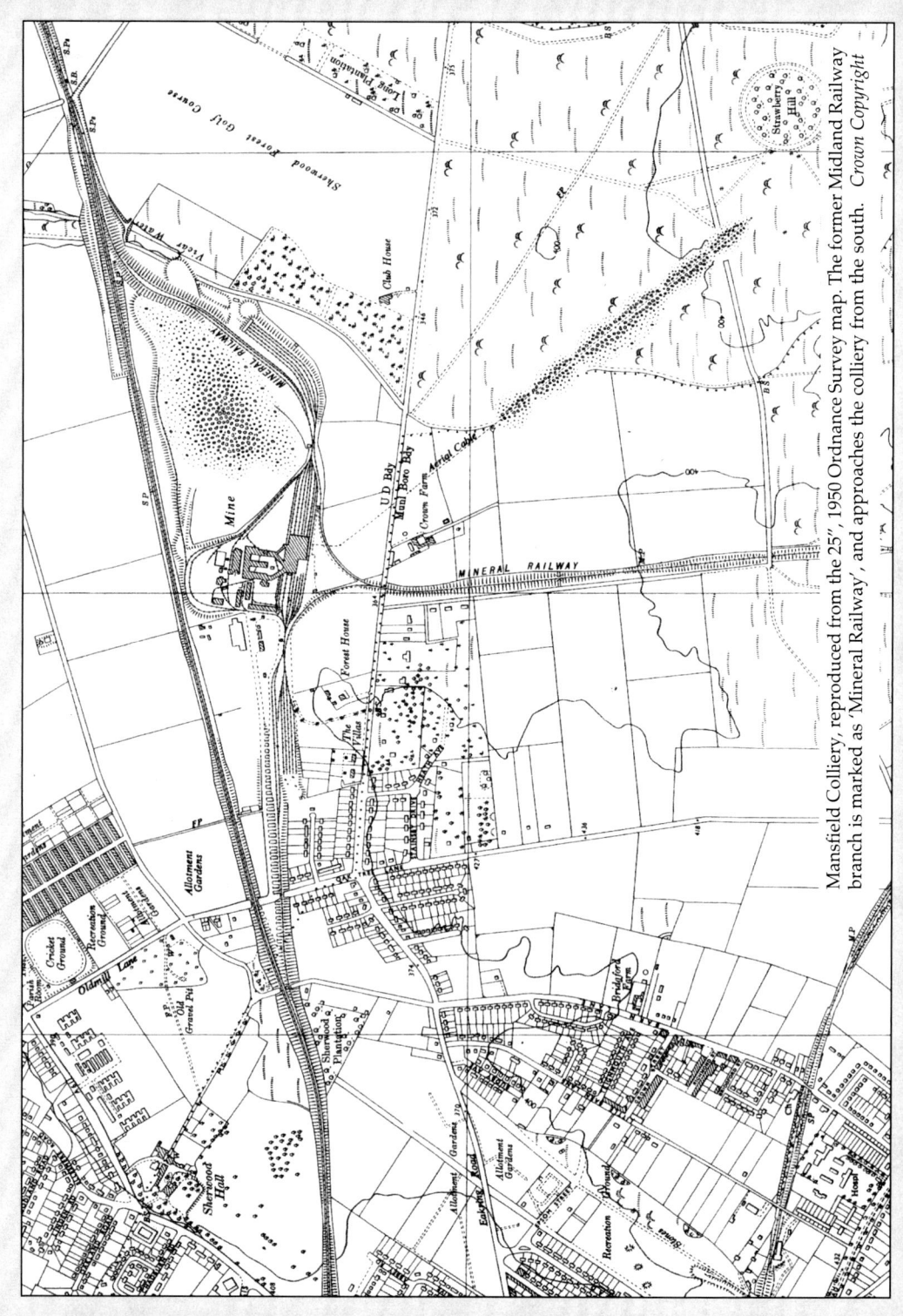

Mansfield Colliery, reproduced from the 25″, 1950 Ordnance Survey map. The former Midland Railway branch is marked as 'Mineral Railway', and approaches the colliery from the south. *Crown Copyright*

Mansfield Colliery signal box. *Author's Collection*

Closure of the line west of Mansfield Colliery and another special

In June 1966 general freight services were withdrawn and the goods yard at Mansfield closed. No purpose was served, as a result, in keeping the line open to the west of Mansfield. It was closed from just to the west of Mansfield (Crown Farm) Colliery in January 1968 and the track removed. Before this closure, on 13th August, 1966, the RCTS organized a rail trip. This started from Waterloo and carried over 500 passengers. At Nottingham Victoria a class '8F' 2-8-0 No. 48197 took the train forward along the Great Central main line to Kirkby South Junction where it diverged onto the Mansfield Railway to Clipstone West. A number of engine changes followed as it went via Rotherham, Wath and Penistone before returning directly to Nottingham Victoria, via Sheffield and thence to London Marylebone. This was the last train to cover the down line of the Mansfield Railway. It will be seen that this was not, however, the last special to use the line, at least in part. In August 1970, a significant severance was made when the bridge which had carried the line over the Nottingham-Mansfield Road was demolished. Mansfield Central station became a warehouse for a time but on 11th January, 1971, at a meeting of the Mansfield Town Improvement Committee, it was resolved to clear the site of the line from Pelham Street to Littleworth; the section which included Mansfield Central station. A grant was received for the reclamation of this land and the Mansfield Brewery, seeking to extend its premises, bought part of the area. The work was started almost immediately, although the station building remained for a time, standing in splendid isolation, once the adjoining embankments were removed and presenting a very bizarre sight as it towered above Great Central Road. By 1972 it had gone.

Mansfield Concentration sidings.

Jack Cupit

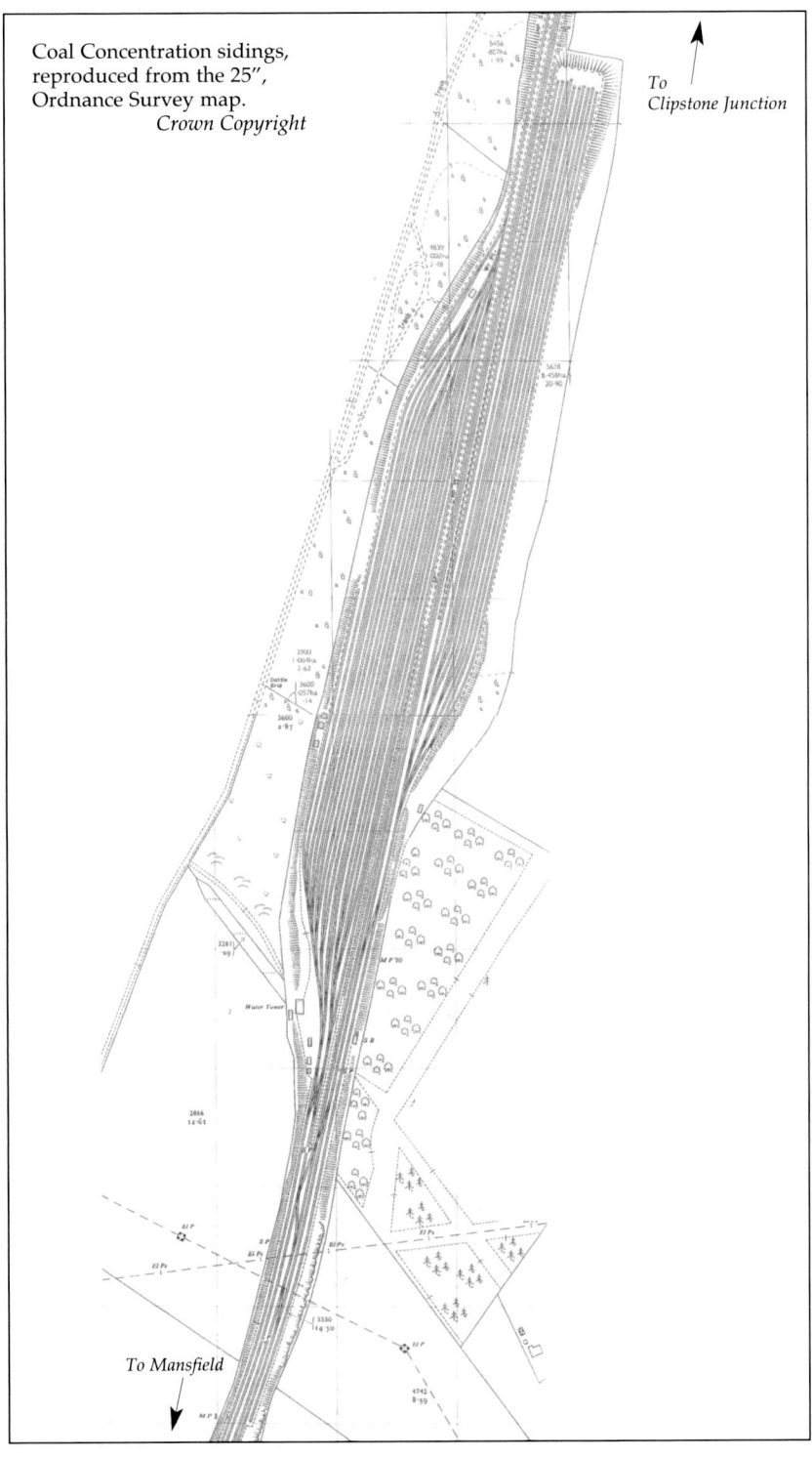

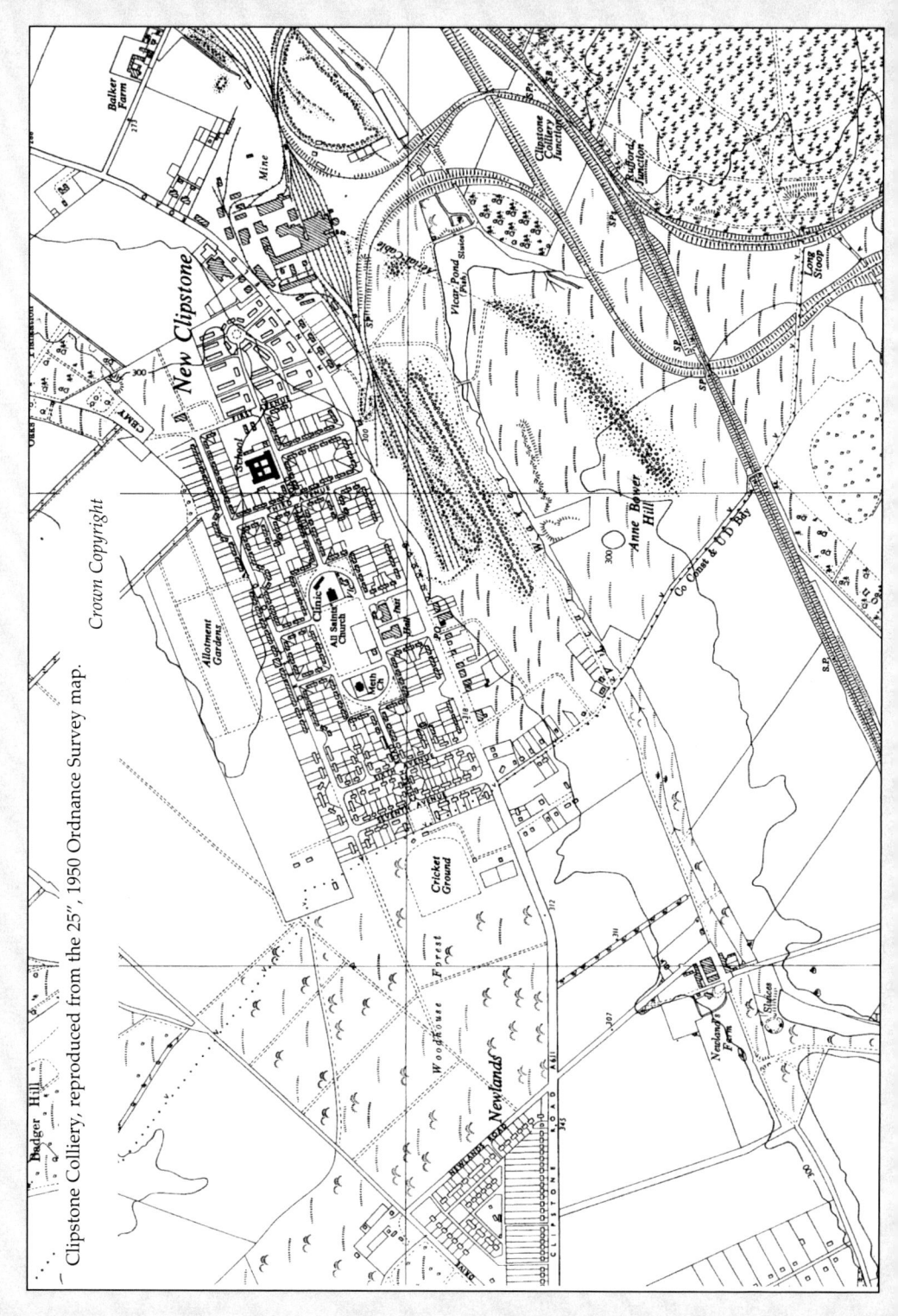

Clipstone Colliery, reproduced from the 25", 1950 Ordnance Survey map.

Crown Copyright

THE MANSFIELD RAILWAY

The line continues to serve the collieries

To the east of Mansfield Colliery it was a very different story. The line now became used exclusively for the transportation of coal, ironically, perhaps, simply serving the purpose for which the original promoters had intended. Nationalization also came to be virtually synonymous with rationalization in some areas and this is what happened at the collieries of the East Midlands as far as rail links were concerned when nationalization occurred. Until this time, Mansfield, Clipstone, Rufford, Blidworth and Bilsthorpe collieries were being served by two companies, the LMS and LNER. Under British Railways Board (BRB) policy it was resolved to effect economies by retaining, where practical, only one of these links. The 'single servicing' of collieries resulted in the ex-LNER connection being retained. The exceptions were Rufford and Clipstone which retained both. In the 1970s there was a peak in the production of coal. In order to meet the considerable demands of power stations, in particular, a system of working using so-called merry-go-round trains was introduced. In this a locomotive, usually in the Nottinghamshire area a class '47' diesel, was in effect permanently coupled to a set of wagons because no shunting would be carried out. These wagons had a capacity of 32 tons each and there were 30 in a train. The wagons could be loaded and unloaded automatically whilst the train was moving and at the loading and unloading points there was a loop which meant the train could move forward, continuously.

Mansfield Colliery was turning out 2,460 tons each day in this period. This coal was leaving on three or four trains and some used the merry-go-round system. Cottom and West Burton power stations received 1,800 tons of this each day with the rest going to Manchester and London.

Blidworth Colliery was yielding 2,500 tons each day with 2,000 tons leaving on merry-go-round trains for Didcot and Cottom power stations with the other 500 tons being taken by conventional loading to the Coventry Homefire Plant, the British Sugar Corporation and domestic use in the south of England.

A Brush type '2' A1A-A1A (later class '31') is seen just after leaving Clipstone Concentration Sidings swinging onto the Shirebrook/Langwith line on 24th September, 1966.   *Author*

An English Electric type '3' (later class '37') hauls a Newcastle-Bournemouth train through Kirkby South Junction on the former Great Central line. In the distance a Brush type '2' (later class '31') can be seen on a train of empty mineral wagons. The Leen Valley Extension curves away to the right. *Author's Collection*

Bilsthorpe Colliery was sending out 4,000 tons each day on four or five trains using the merry-go-round principle although some had also to use conventional loading because at this time the system was not fully automated. This coal went to the power stations at High Marnham, Cottam and West Burton with trains leaving at 02.30 08.34, 11.30 16.30 and 19.30.

As far as the collieries which retained double servicing were concerned Clipstone Colliery was producing 4,460 tons each day and the former Mansfield Railway moved 360 tons of this with 200 tons going to Garston Dock and the rest for domestic use. Rufford Colliery was turning out 2,500 tons each day with 2,000 tons being taken out by the former Mansfield Railway to Cottam and West Burton power stations.

The former Mansfield Railway was certainly proving its worth in terms of the aspirations of its founders with over 50,000 tons being moved out from the collieries each week.

A surprise development

The future could not have looked brighter but events were to take what, for many, was an unexpected turn. The mining industry went into a period of considerable unrest and with no resolution to demands in sight the miners decided to take industrial action to achieve their objectives. The outcome was that in the winter of 1978 and into 1979 the country was crippled by a fuel crisis. There were lengthy power cuts and some parts of industry virtually ground to a halt. Some years later, even when this was all over, it seemed to many there was political retribution in the air and within only a short space of years, moves were taken to run down Britain's coal industry. Widespread closure of mines was proposed. All attempts to resist the implementation of this action proved futile in the face of a determined regime; the National Coal Board would be assigned to history. Mansfield Colliery was closed in 1988, Blidworth, the following year and Rufford in 1993. Amongst all this, another special was run. In 1989, whilst all this was happening, a remarkable excursion was organized before the curtain finally came down on what was left of the Mansfield Railway. In the centenary year of the Institute of Mining Engineers, the Institute ran, in April, a train, made up of dmus, a trip which took in what was left of the Mansfield Railway and its associated branches. As noted previously, by this time, Mansfield (Crown Farm) Colliery had already closed but Clipstone, Rufford and Bilsthorpe were still open. The excursion, after joining the line at Clipstone, was therefore able to travel across the majority of the section that remained of the Mansfield Railway to the east of Mansfield and the branches. It is noted how the Concentration Sidings, now was unnecessary (following the introduction of merry-go-round workings) had been lifted and that the signal box controlling them had closed in July, three years previously. The journey, after a reversal at the point where the Mansfield Colliery had been, was next down the Rufford branch. After calling at Bilsthorpe, Blidworth and finally Rufford the excursion returned to Clipstone and then went forward to Edwinstowe. After these closures, two of the group served by the old Mansfield Railway, then remained open for a time under the private ownership of RJB but the reprieve proved short lived with Bilsthorpe, which had originally been closed in 1994 but was then reopened, finally closing in 1997. However, at Clipstone, mining did continue. This mine, which was closed by British Coal in 1993, was reopened by RJB in 1994 under 'lease licence'. Until May 2003 there were still viable reserves and UK Coal (formerly RJB) worked these. Some 11,000 tonnes of coal left the colliery each week by rail for Trent Valley power stations. There were two trains each day. This development meant a very small section of the old Mansfield Railway was fitted with colour light signalling, from Clipstone Colliery to the junction with what used to be the LD&ECR. Even so, this section was, in reality, just a spur from the main line. In April 2003 it was announced that Clipstone Colliery would close and the last coal was taken out on 17th April. With the closure of Clipstone Colliery it was assumed in some quarters that closure of the whole line was inevitable. The Mansfield Railway, so closely linked to the collieries it served, could only have survived if the collieries also survived.

UK Coal initially retained the use of the old Rufford Colliery site and stock yard and these continued to be serviced by the line from the Clipstone triangle and along the branch which used to serve Rufford Colliery. However, by 2007, movement along this section was very spasmodic with apparently no regular workings. During the same year there were acts of vandalism and theft, probably as a result of this being an isolated area. Signalling equipment was stolen and track was taken up and removed, no doubt in view of the price that it was possible to get for scrap metal. Such was the damage that when later in the year railfreight company EWS considered accessing the site this proved impractical. There was a move to try and put the line in order again following this decision but although Network Rail started work between Clipstone and Rufford Junction the following year it was abandoned when more theft and acts of vandalism occurred. The next move to be anticipated was the removal of the Clipstone triangle and implementation of this would mean the former Mansfield Railway (or what was left of it) would be totally cut off.

LD&ECR class 'D' 0-6-4T, carrying its LNER number, 6150, is seen on shed at Tuxford on 8th May, 1946. *H.C. Casserley*

'O4/3' class 2-8-0 No. 63668 hauling empty steel-carrying wagons from Woodford to Frodingham heads from Kirkby South Junction towards Kirkby-in-Ashfield (Central).
Phil Robinson/John Hitchins Collection

Chapter Six

Motive power

The comparatively late opening date of the Mansfield Railway resulted in the use of motive power which consisted of classes coming from the latter period of steam and many of the types in use when the line opened saw out the days of steam. It would be unwise to claim that what follows is an exhaustive list of all the types of motive power (steam and diesel) which used this line, given that there were so many 'visitors'. The following survey has been compiled from a considerable amount of correspondence and a number of sources and the information here is well chronicled.

Initially, the GCR was the operating company and as far as freight was concerned, locomotives came from the sheds at Langwith and Tuxford. Robinson's engines were amongst some of the first to appear as well as ex-LD&ECR engines. (A photograph in an article in the *Railway Magazine* in 1915 depicts an ex-LD&ECR 0-6-4T working empty wagons at Mansfield Colliery.) Robinson's 'J11' class 0-6-0 (sometimes referred to as 'Pom-Poms') worked on the line and these were followed by his 0-8-0 engines. In later years coal was hauled by the class '8K' 2-8-0s and these were still being used when steam workings ceased. This class became the 'O4' class under the LNER and these engines were joined by the Gresley 'O1' and 'O2' 2-8-0 classes. After World War II 'Austerity' 2-8-0s helped with the workings, hauling general freight as well as coal and towards the end BR class '9F' 2-10-0s hauled some of the mineral trains. The line was a through route especially for steel from North Lincolnshire and fish from Grimsby giving rise to an even greater variety of motive power. The 'B1' and 'K3' class locomotives together with 'K2s' were also used on summer holiday and excursion trains (including colliery specials) which took the people who lived in the vicinity of the line, not least the many miners and their families, off to the seaside, especially the east coast, for well earned summer holidays or days out. Latterly the fish trains were hauled by 'Britannia' class Pacifics which were seeing out some of their last days.

Local passenger traffic saw a medley of, mainly, tank engines with a lot of comings and goings (and returns) over the years. Annesley initially provided the engines. Members of Robinson's 'C14' class 4-4-2T ('9N' under the GCR) were used and then 0-4-4T LNER 'G3s' (designed by Wilson Worsdell). Later, after the Grouping, Annesley 'A5' class 4-6-2Ts (designed by Robinson) appeared but by the mid-1920s these had gone and the 'C14s' had returned. These were in use until the mid-1930s working from Arkwright Street shed. There is also evidence, provided by a photograph taken by T.G. Hepburn, of a Goose Fair train at Nottingham Victoria station and destined for the Mansfield line, that during the 1920s the Robinson 'L1' class (later designated 'L3', following the introduction of Thompson's 2-6-4T in 1945, which became the 'L1' class) allocated to Annesley, were used occasionally on the passenger runs, although these locomotives were intended as 'freight' tank engines. Annesley then relinquished its position as far as passenger engines were concerned and Colwick took over in 1938. In the 1930s

During 1952 'O2/3' class 2-8-0 No. 63968 is seen on a train of empty wagons used for carrying steel from Newport, south Wales, to Frodingham as it climbs away from Kirkby South Junction towards Kirkby-in-Ashfield Central. *Frank Ashley*

WD 'Austerity' class 2-8-0 No. 90492 passes through Kirkby-in-Ashfield Central with an up goods in the early 1950s. *T.G. Hepburn/Rail Archive Stephenson*

G.N. Ivatt's 'C12' class 4-4-2Ts made their debut and in the 1940s Ivatt's 'N1' class 0-6-2Ts were given a role in the scheme of things. 'A5s' also made a return appearance together with Robinson's 'C13' class 4-4-2Ts. In 1941 an interesting decision was made to bring in 'Metropolitan' 4-4-4 tanks ('H2' class) and for a time these hauled the local passenger trains from Nottingham to Edwinstowe. (No. 6420 was seen in April 1943 and No. 6419 in July of the same year.) Accounts suggest that these engines proved quite unsuitable for the run. Their large cylinders, which enabled them to make fast starts from the suburban stations on the lines in the London area, where they had been previously, were inadequate for the steeper gradients and they frequently stopped, short of steam especially in the Hollinwell and Annesley areas, with the long haul up to Kirkby-in-Ashfield Central being too much for them. Sometimes they would stop short of the platform and a story is told of a popular comedian of the period called Stainless Steven. He was appearing at the theatre in Mansfield and travelled on the train each day to do so. He made a quip that the station masters had to put bread poultices on the platforms to draw the trains into the stations. It seems the LNER Directors heard about this and took exception to the remark. They insisted that he make an apology!

Although local passenger trains were usually hauled by tank engines there were exceptions and Gresley's 'J6' class 0-6-0 appeared on this turn occasionally. After the 'H2s' had gone, the Gresley 'N2' class 0-6-2T class took over (Nos. 9550, 9552, 9555, 9560 were the mainstay). Following the 1950 accident, referred to in Chapter Five, the 'N2s' were moved away. It was now the turn of ex-GER 'N7s'. It is reported that these engines were unpopular with drivers because they had the Westinghouse brake system. Latterly, and until the end of local services, Robinson 'A5' 4-6-2T engines took over. As it happened, the last local passenger train was hauled by a Thompson 'L1' 2-6-4T. When Mansfield enjoyed a Marylebone link in the 1920s, 'D9' class 4-4-0s were used and the Mansfield through coach was a GCR composite corridor brake. It actually carried a board with the letters painted white, shaded black with a red background 'Mansfield-Nottingham-Leicester-London Marylebone'.

A local passenger train heading towards Kirkby South Junction and Nottingham, hauled by 'A5' class 4-6-2T No. 69809 crossing the Pinxton branch.   *Frank Ashley*

'C12' class 4-4-2T No. 4528 enters Warsop station with the 4.00 pm Chesterfield to Lincoln passenger train on 8th May, 1946. *H.C. Casserley*

'C13' class 4-4-2T No. 67427 departs Edwinstowe on 11th April, 1955.
T.G. Hepburn/Rail Archive Stephenson

In 1941 ex-Metropolitan Railway 'H2' class 4-4-4Ts Nos. 6415-6422 were transferred to Nottinghamshire to work primarily Nottingham suburban lines and Chesterfield to Lincoln services. Designed by Charles Jones and erected by Kerr, Stuart & Co. Ltd during 1920/21, these became the last examples of 4-4-4T in Britain. This view shows No. 6421 in 1939 before transfer from Metropolitan line duties. *Locomotive Publishing Co.*

An example of a 'D9' class 4-4-0. This type was used when Mansfield enjoyed a link to Marylebone in the 1920s. *Real Photographs*

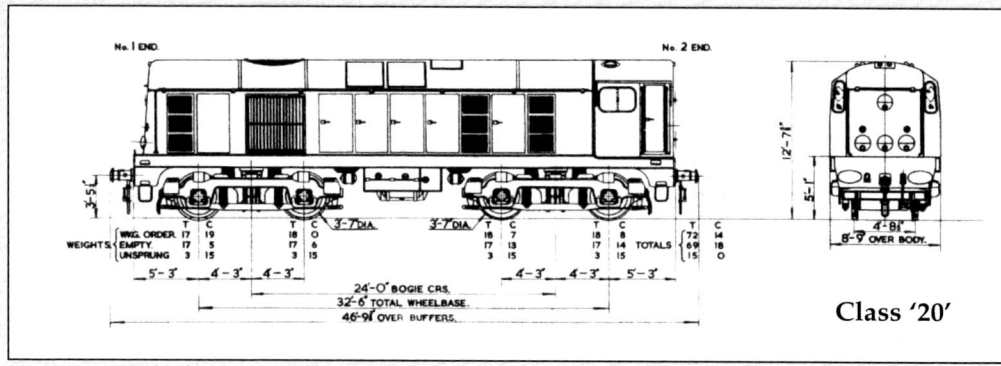

Class '20'

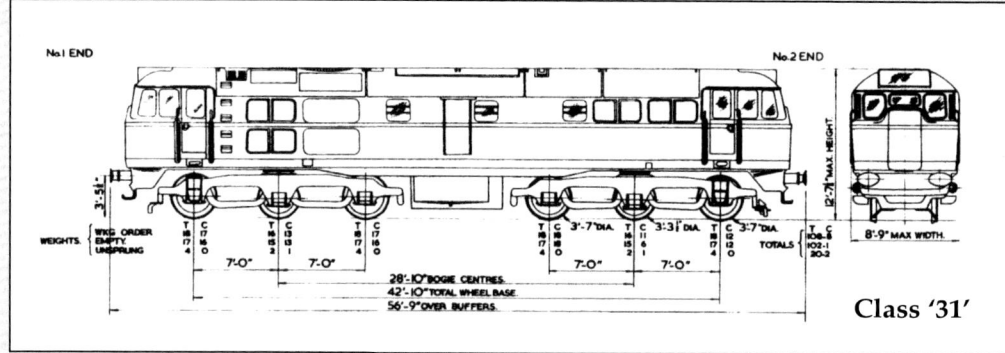

Class '31'

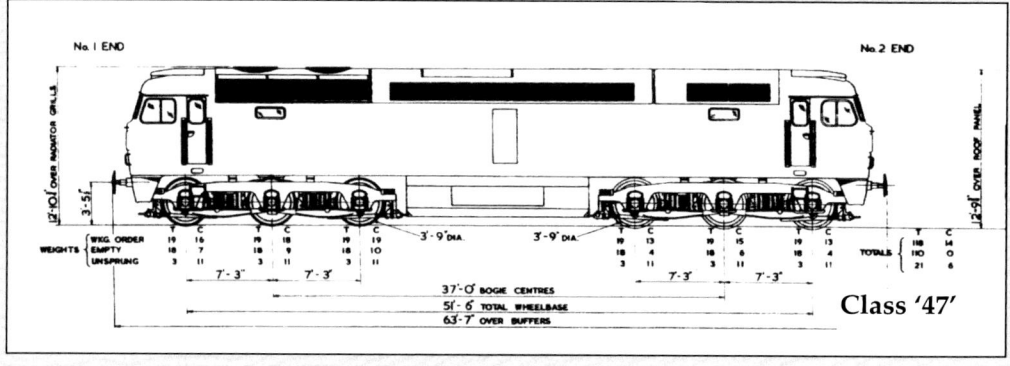

Class '47'

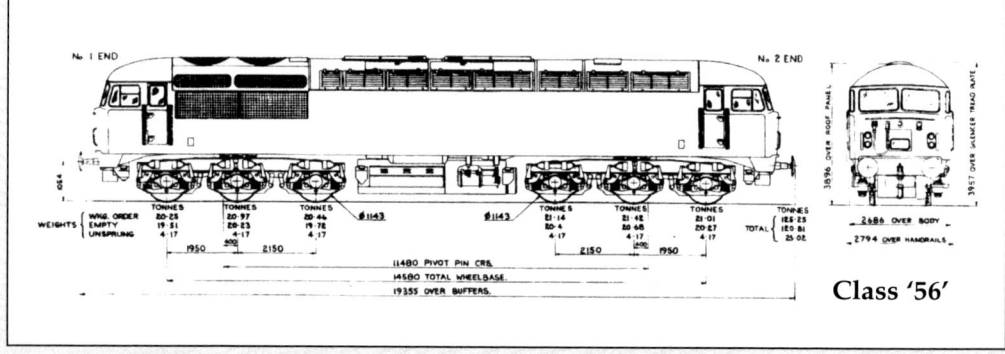

Class '56'

MOTIVE POWER

'C2' class 4-4-2 No. 3271.   *Real Photographs*

Sometimes a 'B8' class was used on this service and later Robinson's 'D10' ('Directors') were rostered. The Atlantics, 'C2' class, made appearances. It is reported that,

> At this time [1927] the Leeds-Bournemouth was actually a Leeds to Nottingham via the Mansfield line and consisted of three coaches which were attached to the Newcastle to Bournemouth at Nottingham Victoria. Similarly, in the reverse direction, three coaches were taken off the Bournemouth to Newcastle. A small Atlantic locomotive was a regular engine on this turn, *Henry Oakley* being one of these engines. To fill in the time between arrival at Nottingham at 12.17 pm and departure at 4.58 pm, the locomotive was used on a short distance local passenger service.

Towards the end of the steam era when there was a Midland Region influence, a Stanier '5MT' 4-6-0 hauled a daily parcels train which involved a certain amount of shunting in the goods yard at Mansfield and one unusual sighting reported was GWR 'Hall' class No. 5979 *Cruckton Hall* on a ballast train. By this time 'Britannia' class locomotives could be seen at the Concentration Sidings; No. 70037 was seen there on 15th December, 1960 and No. 70039 on a train of empties from Whitemoor on 5th December of the same year. The 'Britannia' class locomotives were too large to use the turntable at Langwith and were therefore turned on the Clipstone triangle. Eventually, steam gave way to diesel. One unusual visitor was a Clayton diesel. This was loaned to Shirebrook for driver training purposes, following a batch of these locomotives being transferred from Scotland to Staveley in June 1965. Initially, coal trains were hauled by Brush class '31' (then type '2') locomotives, formerly in their distinctive green livery with narrow white stripes. Langwith steam depot was closed in October 1965 and these locomotives were stabled at the new diesel depot at Shirebrook. The virtual monopoly of this class was broken by the arrival of Brush type '4' (later designated class '47') diesels working the merry-go-round trains and these classes were among some of the last to work the line. Other classes of diesel which made appearances were '20', '56', '58' and '66'.

Hawthorn, Leslie 0-4-0ST *Diana* (Works No. 3912 of 1937) at Mansfield Colliery.
Author's Collection

Hawthorn, Leslie 0-4-0ST *Clipstone No. 2* (Works No. 3630 of 1925) at Clipstone.
Author's Collection

Coaching stock

Coaching stock for local trains consisted mainly of three or four non-corridor coaches, although later there were exceptions and the LNER did introduce a composite coach into some trains (making a five-coach set) and this coach was usually placed in the centre of the formation. The corridor was only in the coach itself (in other words, with no connection to other coaches) and there were two lavatories in the centre. One was first-class, the other, third class with no access between the two halves on the coach. Clearly, on the through trains, a wide variety of stock was used. For example, it is reported that through coaches on the Leeds to Bournemouth trains (mentioned earlier) included GCR corridor compo brake and GCR corridor thirds with GNR corridor thirds being incorporated on Friday and Saturday only trains. On the return train Southern Railway (SR) corridor composite brake and corridor thirds were included although there are also reports that LNER and SR stocks were mixed on each train, suggesting it is not possible to give a definitive statement for all occasions. The Newcastle to Bournemouth trains were worked by fixed rakes of coaches, one set provided by each company.

Motive power at collieries

Each of the collieries had resident locomotives for moving and shunting wagons around the plant. Before the nationalization of the coal industry and the formation of the National Coal Board (1947), these locomotives belonged to the company which usually owned a group of collieries and there seems to have been a tendency to move locomotives around from time to time. The locomotives were either 0-4-0 or 0-6-0 saddle tanks and came from a variety of makers. An idea of the range can be found in the listings for the period just before 1947 and nationalization.

Bolsover Colliery Company

Mansfield (Crown Farm) Colliery
Sir Henry	0-4-0ST	Yorkshire Engine Co.
Mansfield No. 2	0-4-0ST	Hawthorn, Leslie
Thoresby No. 1	0-4-0ST	Hawthorn, Leslie
Diana	0-4-0ST	Hawthorn, Leslie

Clipstone Colliery
Clipstone No. 1	0-4-0ST	Hawthorn, Leslie
Clipstone No. 2	0-4-0ST	Hawthorn, Leslie

Rufford Colliery
Rufford No. 1	0-6-0ST	Manning, Wardle
Rufford No. 2	0-4-0ST	Hawthorn, Leslie

Stanton Ironworks Company

Bilsthorpe Colliery
Bilsthorpe No. 1   0-6-0ST   Hawthorn, Leslie
Bilsthorpe No. 2   0-6-0ST   Andrew Barclay

Newstead Colliery Company

Blidworth Colliery
Blidworth No. 1   0-6-0ST   Avonside Engine Co.
Billum   0-6-0ST   Avonside Engine Co.

Avonside Engine Co 0-6-0ST *Blidworth No. 1* at Blidworth Colliery on 18th April, 1949.
J.B. Latham

Chapter Seven

Some recollections of the line

Eric Brailsford

When work started on this manuscript Eric was still alive. As a small boy he had witnessed the opening of the railway:

> From an early age I first heard the 'peep peep' of the little engines busy in what turned out to be the marshalling yard and of the one that brought the debris from the cutting being dug out from Sutton station to Kirkby-in-Ashfield.

On the opening:

> The first train was from Nottingham to Ollerton, where the distinguished guests, shareholders and executives had lunch at the Hop Pole. I forgot at what time they came back but a whole lot of people gathered in Great Central Road. I saw it all from grandad's back yard. The engine carried an array of flags on the smoke box and the train stopped in the station and filled up with water.

During World War I:

> I remember very vividly seeing the soldiers being brought into Mansfield station GC. They didn't come down through the station they just jumped down the embankments.
> To visit Auntie Phoebe at Sutton cost 1½d. on the tram but I used to save up my 2d. per week pocket money until I had got 3½d. I would then go to the station and go to Sutton by train. Very often I was the only passenger; the 2.10 from Mansfield. I came back by tram.

R. Beeton

> I well remember going on summertime excursions to the Lincolnshire coast, usually behind a Doncaster 'K3' from Mansfield Central via Lincoln at a cost of 4s. 6d. per adult - full day; 2s. 6d. - half day (after mid-day) and 1s. 6d. - evening (after 4 pm). All returning departures between 11.30 pm and midnight.
> The Nottingham service to Victoria was very popular especially with Saturday shoppers, cutting the Midland journey time by over ten minutes.
> Carrington station would be opened specially for the Goose Fair.
> Coal trains, having been assembled at Clipstone Concentration Sidings would struggle to get traction behind a Robinson 'O4' or being checked at the Mansfield station distant signal (which was adjacent to my back yard) and me as a 4 to 5 year old waving and shouting to the footplate crew, who, having nothing better to do until 'getting a green' were waving and shouting back. My sole ambition at that time was to become an engine driver; something I never achieved until retirement when I did footplate service on preserved railways.

John Hitchens

Around 1950, a favourite place to watch trains was in Kirkby Portland Park. At one point the GCR main line and the Mansfield line crossed the Midland Pinxton branch on two parallel bridges. After the passage of 'The South Yorkshireman' express, the signals would go 'off' on the Mansfield branch and a 'B1' running tender first would cross Kirkby South Junction and run down the Mansfield line. For some weeks this engine was 61209, an Annesley 'B1', immaculate in apple green with black lining and 'British Railways' written out in full on the tender. As the engine turned the corner in the cutting towards Kirkby Central Station it was time to go home to arrive before supper at 9 o' clock. I cannot recall being late. The engine was on its way to take over one of the fish trains from Grimsby en route for Banbury.

The Central Station at Kirkby had a more welcoming booking hall; a wooden floor helped and the walls were adorned with framed certificates denoting the station had won the 1st Class Prize in the Station Garden Competition. Being away from the main road it was quieter. The station gardens were a sight to behold and there was also birdsong. No rush or hassle.

Postscript

There is still some evidence left of the old Mansfield Railway but this gets less and less. In the section to the west of the site of Mansfield Colliery especially in and around Mansfield, most of the evidence of a former railway line has been obliterated by development. There are signs in the Kirkby area, where the cutting remains in which the railway climbed away from the GCR main line. The high embankment, which carried the GCR main line and the Mansfield Railway, at an even higher level, across the River Erewash, has virtually disappeared, although the boundary fencing where the line entered a cutting as it curved its way towards Kirkby-in-Ashfield Central can be seen but an industrial estate occupies the former station site. In spite of this, the remnants of one end of a footbridge remain. The approach road to the industrial estate is named 'New Line Road' and this no doubt relates to the Mansfield Railway often being referred to as 'The Central' and as a consequence the 'New Line'. The cutting through which the line approached Sutton-in-Ashfield Central has been filled in but the route can be traced as the infill carries a footpath up to the point where it meets the A38 road, which also follows the former line as far as Sutton Central. The station was situated on the north side of the traffic lights. The A38 diverges and the original embankment can be seen, carrying a footpath to Coxmoor Road. There are further sections where only the boundary fencing remains. To the east of Mansfield there are places where the old track bed is clearly visible and the brick pillars which held the massive water tower, used at the Concentration Sidings, still stand; rather forlorn but still a dominant feature and reminder of the busy activity this section once saw.

The collieries, too, have virtually disappeared, except for Clipstone, closed in 2003, where there is a move to ensure that the headstocks, 210 ft high (the highest in Europe) which carried the winding gear and which were installed in 1955 will remain as a monument to a once flourishing industry.

So, Old King Coal *was* dethroned and his attendant, the railway, has also been banished. And there is an irony in the story; a twist in the tail. The Midland, at the end of the day, has emerged as the victor. The old rival, once also closed through Mansfield, is now open again as The Robin Hood Line. Sadly, 'The Central' cannot hope for such a resurrection.

Appendix One

Acts of Parliament

1910	26th July	Act for the building of the Railway
1910	28th October	Act for the GCR to work the line
1914	8th July	Act for (i) the western curve at Clipstone
		(ii) branches to Clipstone and Rufford Collieries
1917	24th May	Act for raising further capital
1919	July	Act for a branch to serve Blidworth Colliery (the original Bill had also included the Bilsthorpe branch but this section was withdrawn).

Appendix Two

Opening sequence

Mansfield Colliery to Clipstone 16th June, 1913 – One observer notes that the first coal train left for Immingham on 6th June 'with regular services starting 10 days later'

Mansfield to Mansfield Colliery 2nd June, 1914

Kirkby to Mansfield 4th September, 1916

The line opened to passenger traffic on 2nd April, 1917.

The company took over the Concentration Sidings near Clipstone Colliery (usually referred to as Mansfield Concentration Sidings) from the contractors on 1st January, 1918.

Rufford branch and the western curve opened in 1918.

Bilsthorpe had a temporary line opened in 1925 to assist with the sinking of the mine. The branch opened in 1927 shortly before the colliery started full production.

The Blidworth branch was virtually complete by 1928 but following the postponement of the opening of the colliery was not fully completed until 1934. Operated under 'lease licence' until April 2003. The closure of this colliery brought to an end regular workings.

Langwith Junction shed with 'O4/8' class 2-8-0 No 63840, to the left. An ex-GCR 'J11' class 0-6-0 'Pom Pom' leads the line to the right, with an 'Austerity' 2-8-0 in the centre.

Colour Rail.com/16444

An overall view of Langwith Junction shed on 15th August, 1954. Amongst the engines on view, are Robinson 'J11' 0-6-0 No. 64297, Thompson 'K1' Mogul No. 62055 and Riddles WD 'Austerity' 2-8-0 No. 90043. Langwith shed was to play host to the last surviving GCR engine in BR service, Robinson 'O4/1' 2-8-0 No 63612, which was withdrawn in November 1965. When Langwith Junction shed closed a few months later, in February 1966, the depot's last three engines were three Thompson 'B1s', Nos 61050, 61051 and 61315. *E.V. Fry/Rail Archive Stephenson*

Appendix Three

Langwith Junction and Shirebrook shed allocations

Langwith Junction, May 1951
'O1' and 'O4' class 2-8-0s
O4/1   63577, 63585, 63597, 63627, 63632, 63658, 63683, 63707, 63809
O4/7   63615, 63643, 63758, 63884
O4/2   63644, 63648, 63709
O4/3   63665, 63679, 63703, 63715, 63717, 63724, 63750, 63759, 63765, 63776, 63800,
        63807, 63833, 63840, 63842, 63870, 63900
O4/6   63902, 63908

'J11' and 'J11/3'* 0-6-0s
64281, 64286, 64289, 64297, 64310, 64321, 64358, 64378, 64379*, 64389, 64414, 64418, 64426
64427*

'N5/2' class 0-6-2Ts
69284, 69319, 69323, 69327

'A5/1' class 4-6-2Ts
69812, 69815, 69821

'Q1' class 0-8-0s
69928, 69929

Langwith Junction, October 1964
'O4' class 2-8-0s
O4/3   63636, 63679, 63691, 63697, 63703, 63717, 63732, 63739, 63842, 63850, 63861
        63877
O4/1   63683
O4/7   63843
O4/8   63828, 63882, 63893
O4/6   63902

WD 'Austerity' 2-8-0s
90043, 90088, 90121, 90164, 90190, 90227, 90258, 90266, 90271, 90275, 90292, 90301, 90398,
90418, 90442, 90449

350 hp diesel shunter 0-6-0 (later class '08')
D3325, D3701, D4053, D4057, D4060, D4061, D4066, D4067, D4069, D4085

Shirebrook, November 1975
Class '08' 350 hp diesel shunter
08 022, 08 214, 08 238, 08 255, 08 263, 08 285, 08 287, 08 331, 08 429, 08 523, 08 560, 08 782,
08 869, 08 889

Appendix Four

The collieries served by the railway

Mansfield Bolsover Colliery Co. Opened in 1905
            Closed in 1988
(Crown Farm)   (Served by The Mansfield Railway
                                    from 1913)

Clipstone Bolsover Colliery Co. Opened in 1922
                                    Closed by British Coal in 1993
                                    Opened by RJB Mining in 1994 operated
                                    under 'lease licence' until April 2003.
                                    The closure of this colliery brought to an
                                    end regular workings on the line.

Bilsthorpe Stanton Ironworks Co. Opened in 1928
                                    Closed initially in 1994
                                    Reopened by RJB Mining
                                    Closed in 1997

Blidworth Newstead Colliery Co. Sunk 1924-28
                                    Closed in 1989
             Sheepbridge Coal & Iron Co. Not fully open until 1934
             Staveley Coal & Iron Co.
             (Joint Venture)

Rufford   Bolsover Colliery Co. Opened in 1912/13
                                    Closed in 1993
                                    The use of the site of this colliery and
                                    stockyard had been retained byUK Coal
                                    resulting in a section of the railway also
                                    being retained from Clipstone Junction

Rufford Colliery

Sources, locations and thanks

Sources

Deposited Plans, Bills and Acts of Parliament
Directors Minutes, Mansfield Railway Company.
Directors Minutes, LNER
Shareholders Minutes
Select Committee Minutes
Local newspapers
The Times
Correspondence - both contemporary (with the line) and modern
The RCTS *Railway Observer*
The RCTS *Locomotives of the LNER Part 3a*
Trains Illustrated
GCR, LNER, and BR timetables
A History of Nottinghamshire, A.C. Wood
British Parliamentary Papers. Fuel and Power. Coal. Session 1871
The NRM Archive
The NCB - correspondence
UK Coal
Railtrack/Network Rail

Locations

The National Archives, Kew
The House of Lords Library
The British Library
The Newspaper Library, Colindale
The Nottingham Record Office
Mansfield Museum
Mansfield Public Library
Darlington Railway Centre and Museum

Thanks

I am very grateful for all the help given to me over the years by the staffs of the various records offices and libraries which are listed under 'Sources' in this appendix. Thanks, particularly to Liz Weston, curator of Mansfield Museum.

In addition, I would like to thank the people who wrote to me with information, often from first-hand experience, in particular the late Eric Brailsford who was present when the special Directors' and guests' train for the (second) opening ceremony arrived at Mansfield station.

I am indebted to the late David Dalton for the information on the motive power used at the collieries and Peter Holmes who sent a large number of items, including working timetables and leaflets. Also Bill Taylor who from the outset (and for many years!) has offered help and encouragement.

A very special word of thanks to John Hitchens, of Kirkby-in-Ashfield, and a former school friend (QEGS Mansfield) who provided a considerable number of timetables, manuals, pamphlets, diagrams and the like, which gave a wealth of background information. His encouragement throughout has been greatly appreciated. Thank you also to Russell Rollings for reading and checking the text, and to Ian Kennedy for turning the various elements into a book.

Index

Accidents, 51, 101 *et seq.*
Acts of Parliament, 8, 15, 18, 32-3, 37, 39, 57, 65, 75, 93, 155
Agreement with Great Central Rly, 16 *et seq.*
Annesley, 8, 10, 49, 86 *et seq.*, 97, 143, 154
Bainbridge, E.M., 11, 13, 16 *et seq.*
Baldry, Yerburgh & Hutchinson, 20, 36, 37, 65
Bilsthorpe Colliery and branch, 26, 49, 61, 64 *et seq.*, 75, 79, 81, 85, 91, 139 *et seq.*, 152, 155, 158
Bleak Hills branch, 59
Blidworth Colliery and branch, 59, 61, 70, 72, 75-7, 81, 85, 91, 139 *et seq.*, 152, 155, 158
Board of Trade inspections, 51, 59, 139 *et seq.*
Bolsover Colliery Co., 7, 10, 11, 16, 21, 33, 41, 55, 56, 83, 93, 158
British Railways, 99, 101, 139 *et seq.*, 149, 154
Bus competition, 75, 99, 107, 111
Chadburn, W.J., 11, 13, 16, 17, 22, 53, 71
Clipstone, 8 *et seq.*, 17, 19, 23, 27 *et seq.*, 39 *et seq.*, 51, 54, 56 *et seq.*, 61, 69, 85 *et seq.*, 107, 121, 127, 135, 141, 149
  Army Camp, 37, 39-40, 57 *et seq.*, 61, 64
  Colliery and branch, 23, 29, 33, 36, 37, 39, 41, 55 *et seq.*, 59, 61, 68, 75, 84, 93, 111, 127, 139, 141, 151, 154, 158
  Concentration sidings, 27, 28, 33, 36, 37, 53, 57, 59, 65, 83, 85 *et seq.*, 101, 141, 153, 155
Closure to goods, 135, 141
Closure to passengers, 113, 119
Craven, Thomas, 18, 20, 23, 53, 65, 73
Crown Farm Colliery (*see* Mansfield Colliery)
Davies, Sanders & Swanwick, 19
Dean & Dawson, 67, 77
Duke of Portland, 8 *et seq.*, 13, 17 *et seq.*, 26 *et seq.*, 55, 59
Edwinstowe, 23, 40, 58, 64, 66, 67, 95, 99, 103, 107, 113, 121, 141, 145
Elliott-Cooper, R., 16 *et seq.*, 35-6, 53, 59, 65
Estimated annual revenue (1910), 17
Excursions after passenger closure, 127
Farnsfield (including colliery), 29, 36, 56, 61, 75, 79
'Fast fish' trains, 5, 49, 101, 111, 143
Fay, Sam, 13 *et seq.*, 19, 20, 22, 23, 27, 29, 35, 39, 41, 51, 65, 69, 70
Forest Town, 57, 65, 70, 84
Gibson, J.G., 53-4
Gradient profile, 50
Great Central Rly, 9 *et seq.*, 16 *et seq.*, 27, 29, 33, 35 *et seq.*, 39, 41, 53 *et seq.*, 64 *et seq.*, 73, 83, 93, 143 *et seq.*, 151
Great Northern Rly, 8 *et seq.*, 14 *et seq.*, 20, 26, 28, 33, 54, 55, 83, 93, 119, 151
Greenwood, John, 36
Haig-Brown, Mr, 17, 27, 36, 37, 41, 73
Hodgkinson Trust, 11, 12, 18
Houfton, J.P., 11, 13, 16, 17, 20, 23, 27, 28, 53-5, 58, 65, 69 *et seq.*, 73, 83
House of Lords Select Committee, 12-15

Installation of signalling, 29, 35 *et seq.*
Kirkby-in Ashfield, 8, 9, 11, 12, 20, 23, 26, 28, 33, 41, 56, 57, 64, 66, 72, 77, 83 *et seq.*, 97, 101, 107, 111, 113, 119 *et seq.*, 145, 153 *et seq.*
Kirkby Jn, 23, 29, 33, 41, 49, 71, 83, 93, 135, 154
Lancashire Derbyshire & East Coast Rly, 8, 9, 11 *et seq.*, 16, 20, 67, 85, 121, 141, 143
Lindley, Colonel, 21, 22
London Midland & Scottish Rly, 76, 139 *et seq.*
London & North Eastern Rly, 15, 27, 67, 71 *et seq.*, 75 *et seq.*, 139, 143 *et seq.*
London & North Western Rly, 8, 9
Lord Savile, 23, 26, 29, 33, 56, 59, 61, 75, 79
Manchester Sheffield & Lincolnshire Rly, 8, 9
Mansfield & District Lt Rly, 65
Mansfield Central, 8, 9, 11, 23, 28-9, 33, 36, 39 *et seq.*, 49, 53, 55 *et seq.*, 64 *et seq.*, 70 *et seq.*, 77, 79, 84 *et seq.*, 95 *et seq.*, 101 *et seq.*, 105, 107, 111 *et seq.*, 119 *et seq.*, 127, 135, 145, 149, 153
Mansfield Colliery, 7, 10, 12, 13, 16 *et seq.*, 21, 23, 27, 28, 36, 41, 54, 55, 59, 75, 84, 89 *et seq.*, 93, 103, 111, 135, 139, 141, 143, 151, 154
Mansfield Concentration Sdgs (*see* Clipstone)
Mansfield Corporation, 11, 12, 21 *et seq.*, 33, 71
Mansfield Military Hospital, 97
Mansfield Vicarage, 20 *et seq.*, 29, 51, 68
Mansfield Woodhouse, 8, 66
Marylebone through trains, 5, 14, 35, 72, 86, 91, 145
Midland Railway, 7 *et seq.*, 12, 13, 18, 19, 21, 22, 61, 66, 83, 93, 111, 121, 127, 157 *et seq.*
Mid-Notts Joint Rly, 79, 101
Newstead Colliery Co., 61, 75, 76, 158
Nottingham, 53, 55, 58, 64, 66, 71, 72, 75, 87 *et seq.*, 95 *et seq.*, 101, 107, 113, 119 *et seq.*, 135, 143 *et seq.*, 149, 153
Oakley, Henry, 8
Ollerton, 8, 55, 57, 58, 64, 66, 67, 71, 72, 75, 79, 87 *et seq.*, 95, 101, 107, 113, 121, 153
Opening to goods, 27-8, 36, 41, 54, 155
Opening to passengers, 51, 53-5, 58-9, 155
Pilling, S.W., 18, 20, 53, 65, 71
Railway Communications Committee, 8 *et seq.*, 13
Rufford Colliery and branch, 16, 18, 19, 23, 26, 29, 33, 36, 37, 41, 51, 55 *et seq.*, 59, 61, 65, 75 *et seq.*, 81, 84 *et seq.*, 93, 139 *et seq.*, 151, 155, 158
Rufford Jn, 57, 85, 87
Sanders, H.A., 16, 18, 19, 37, 41, 53, 65, 69, 72, 73
Sherwood Colliery, 9, 10
Smith, B.A., 19, 22, 23
Stanton Ironworks Co., 49, 64, 65, 67, 77, 158
Sutton-in-Ashfield, 8, 11, 23, 57, 64, 66, 70 *et seq.*, 77, 84 *et seq.*, 97, 101, 107, 111, 119 *et seq.*, 153 *et seq.*
Warsop, 23, 71, 72, 77, 87 *et seq.*, 95
Welbeck Colliery, 56, 57, 88
World War I , 5, 37, 56, 58, 67, 70, 85
World War II, 5, 75, 93, 95 *et seq.*, 111, 143